Hidden Treasure

A Workbook to Help You Discover the Amazing Gift of Your Marriage

Robert and Lori Fontana

Dedicated to our parents, John and Paula Mitchell, and Anthony and Evelyn Fontana, who taught us how to love, and to our children and grandchildren, our very visible treasures.

ISBN: 148408537X
ISBN 13: 9781484085370
Library of Congress Control Number: 2013907324
CreateSpace Independent Publishing Platform
North Charleston, South Carolina

Introduction

MARRIAGE IS AN AMAZING GIFT! We, Lori and Robert, have been <u>happily married</u> since 1978; do the math! We wrote, "happily married," not "perfectly married." Of course it has not all been a proverbial bed of roses; there have been many difficult times for sure. However, we not only weathered and survived these challenges, we grew from them. Our difficulties and troubles became occasions for us to work on our marriage (and in the early days, there were many occasions to work on our marriage). We learned through conflict how to be less selfish, more loving, and wiser in our life together.

Most importantly, we could not have succeeded on our own. From the beginning of our relationship, we knew that God had to be at the center and that we needed the support of family and friends especially those who were part of our community of faith. And guess what? We are a marriage success —not a perfect marriage, but a successful one. We have found the "treasure hidden in a field, the pearl of great price" (Matthew 13:44-45).

The kingdom of heaven is like a treasure buried in a field, which a person finds and hides again, and out of joy goes and sells all that he has and buys that field. Again, the kingdom of heaven is like a merchant searching for fine pearls. When he finds a pearl of great price, he goes and sells all that he has and buys it.

We have "sold all that we have" to possess this hidden treasure, meaning that we have committed all of our resources to succeeding in marriage and have refused to allow any person, place, or thing to keep us from doing so. And we have reaped the rewards from this hidden treasure that <u>money cannot buy</u>: a happy life!

How do we know that we are happy? Because joy, love, peace, patience, self-control, generosity,

self-denial—the fruits of a happy life described by St. Paul (Galatians 5:22)—are present in our lives. Not all the time, and not without times of suffering and trauma, but they are present enough for us to say they form a pattern in our lives.

WE REALLY ENJOY BEING MARRIED, and we are not alone! Lots of couples enjoy being married. University of Chicago sociologist Linda Waite and Maggie Gallagher, co-founder of the National Organization for Marriage, in their book *The Case for Marriage* (2000), explain why couples like us enjoy being married. Waite and Gallagher reviewed studies from across the country that compared couples in successful marriages with individuals and couples who are single, divorced, or cohabiting. Couples who are married come out ahead in almost every category.

- *You want to have greater wealth? Succeed in marriage.*
- *You want to live a long life? Succeed in marriage.*
- *You want emotional and physical well-being? Succeed in marriage.*
- *You want healthy children prepared to be successful adults? Succeed in marriage.*
- *You want strong churches, safe neighborhoods, and successful schools? Succeed in marriage.*
- *Last but not least, you want great sex that is thoroughly satisfying and mutually enriching? SUCCEED IN MARRIAGE![1]*

It is absolutely clear that a successful marriage is the proverbial "jackpot" in life. In Christian terms it is "the treasure hidden in a field, the pearl of great price." By this I mean couples who succeed in marriage participate in what Jesus described as the Kingdom of God budding forth on earth. A successful marriage brings about concrete and specific benefits to couples that simply cannot be bought. These benefits mentioned above are the result of two people making the commitment to one another and working on their marriage till death do they part.

Marriage, of course, was not invented by the great religions of the world — including Catholic Christianity. It pre-dates all religions. Judaism, followed by Christianity, has given the world a unique perspective on marriage. Our common faith teaches us that marriage is not merely part of the social, evolutionary biology of the human species. It is an institution given to us by God to help us live out the truth of our existence - we are creatures made in God's image and likeness. We are made to give and receive love and create life in a way remarkably like our Creator (see Genesis 1-2).

This book is about the amazing gift of marriage from the Catholic perspective. It is not a book for Catholics only, but for anyone who wants to be successful in marriage. Because the core principals of a Catholic marriage are universal, anyone practicing them will succeed in marriage. Successful marriages do not just happen. Couples have to be intentional about working on their marriages ever day of every week, year after year. In their book *Bull's-eye Marriage*, my brother and sister-in-law, Francis and Sara Fontana, use the image of targeting the bull's-eye to challenge their readers to "develop a clear concise mental picture of a great marriage and then strive for that."[2]

This is also a workbook for you to use to help you and your spouse discover the great gift of your relationship and give you insights on how to make it better. You will gain the most from this book by reading it together as a couple and doing the couple exercises, relationship assessments, and inventories that are included in each chapter. (A second set of assessments is provided at the end of the book to make it easier for each member of the couple to complete them separately. These may be torn from the book to be completed.)

THIS IS IMPORTANT: The purpose of these couple activities, assessments and inventories is to get you to listen to one another so that you <u>understand</u> each other. It is not to win an argument, persuade your spouse to your point of view, or even problem-solve. (That will come later). The purpose is to help you get in the habit of listening carefully to one another so that you fully understand each other before you begin to problem-solve. Be sure to invite one another to explain any aspects of the inventories that show differences between the two of you, or that one of you simply does not understand.

Lastly, this book includes our marriage experiences when it needs to. We will tell our story as it seems appropriate and helpful — and encourage you to tell each other your stories.

If you are in a successful marriage, you have won the "lottery of life!" You are rich beyond measure. And the greatest benefit of your marriage success is something that money could never buy: the peace of mind, friendship, personal satisfaction, and joy that come from the giving and receiving of love over a lifetime with your spouse.

Table of Contents

CHAPTER 1

A Hidden Treasure

"The Kingdom of heaven is like a treasure buried in a field, which a person finds and hides again, and out of joy goes and sells all that she has and buys that field. Again, the kingdom of heaven is like a merchant searching for fine pearls. When he finds a pearl of great price, he goes and sells all that he has and buys it." (Mt 13:44-46)

Yes, my faith is the treasure hidden in a field and the "pearl of great price!" Through a college retreat, I, Lori, was awakened to the awesome love of Jesus for me and every human being. I then began the slow but steady effort to "buy that field and purchase that pearl." I wanted to spend more time with Jesus in prayer so I read the Scriptures, prayed the rosary, and sang hymns of praise. I went to the nursing home to visit the "Jesus" who lived there among the elderly and poor. I received the Eucharist, confessed my sins, and became part of a vibrant Catholic student community.

Many years later, most of these years as a married woman, I'm convinced that my marriage, too, is that hidden treasure alluded to in Scripture. My marriage in Christ, a sacrament of life and love, is worth whatever sacrifice is necessary to make

it work. It takes all the faith, hope, and love that Jesus has given me to love and serve my spouse and family.

Marriage comes at a great cost – EVERYTHING! The happily-ever-after scenario from the fairy tales is just that; a fairy tale, unless <u>both spouses</u> are willing to risk everything – their egos, independence, self-centeredness, personal hopes and dreams, etc. – in order to become one in Christ. Thankfully, we have a lifetime to do this because it does take a lifetime for couples to:

- *value one another as persons*
- *accept each other as they truly are*
- *speak to one another in love and truth*
- *forgive one another daily*
- *listen to one another*
- *pray together on a regular basis*
- *seek God's will for their marriage*
- *sacrifice for one another*
- *give and receive physical love and respect*
- *welcome children with graciousness*
- *work together in raising children*
- *form in their children a Christian character*
- *manage money, sharing with those in need*
- *save for the future*
- *mature with one another over life's changes*
- *care for one another in sickness and tragedy*
- *help one another face death with faith, hope, and love.*

Marriage is the hidden treasure. It demands of us every ounce of energy, every skill at communicating, and every reserve within our hearts to live up to the promise we made in our marriage vows: "to love, to be true, and to honor."

What is the "hidden treasure" that could be worth such a sacrificial way of life? Peace! In John's Gospel

(14:27, 16:33) we read, *"Peace I leave with you; my peace I give to you. Not as the world gives do I give it to you…I have told you this that you might have peace in me…In the world you will have trouble, but take courage, I have conquered the world."*

Sadly, many people choose not to give their marriage much attention. The television, computer, personal hobbies, favorite sports teams, the local mall, and work get more attention than do our marriages. How many of us, with all the advantages of modern life, are wracked with stress, worry, and fear? What would we give for peace? It is a gift that comes from buying that hidden treasure buried in the field of life.

My in-laws taught me this lesson in ways that I will never forget. My mother-in-law, Evelyn, suffered from depression. This disease was managed later in her life. But when I first met her, I in my mid-20's, she in her late 40's, Evelyn experienced long months when depression had the upper hand; she was often a tormented, despairing woman.

Tony and Evelyn Fontana on their wedding day.

In the midst of the trauma that depression brought into their lives, one constant was my father-in-law, Tony, and his love for Evelyn. And Evelyn deeply loved Tony. Some days he would have to help Evelyn through the day step-by-step, dressing, cooking, eating, and sleeping. Their covenant to one another was stretched and tested, but never broken. When the depression subsided, their commitment bore great peace, joy, and love — the fruits of sacrifice and enduring commit-

ment. For them, their marriage was truly the pearl for which they were willing to pay a great price.

Marriage, interestingly enough, is not simply about the couple's loving one another and their children, should they have any. It is about their being a building block for the Kingdom of God on earth. Keep in mind that Jesus spoke of a kingdom that was breaking into this world, into time and space, and he even taught us to pray, "thy kingdom come, thy will be done on earth as it is in heaven."

Jesus did not come just to save our souls for heaven. Jesus came to bring heaven to earth. One of the fundamental ways that we continue His work of Kingdom-building is by succeeding in marriage. Marriage is a fundamental building block for the Kingdom of God on earth and, as such, it is foundational for the building of a just society. God uses marriage to help couples be a power for good in the world and to raise children who will do the same.

Tony's and Evelyn's marriage was not just about them. Their relationship gave them a foundation of faith, hope, and love that enabled them to be great parents – they raised seven boys – and effective music educators. But Tony and Evelyn taught more than music! They reached out to high-school-aged youth who were having trouble during the teenage years. Many came to their home late at night and on weekends for help with problems at home, issues of faith, and, of course, teen love. Their marriage gave Tony and Evelyn a stable life from which they could love each other, care for their children, and reach out to young people troubled by life's growing pains.

Couple Exercise *Review the article. Which of the following qualities form a pattern in your life together, meaning which are present most of the time? Love, joy, peace, patience, kindness, generosity, faithfulness, gentleness, self-control*

Which are missing?

What married couples do you know that exhibit these qualities?

CHAPTER 2

The Marriage Jackpot and The Amazing Gift of Your Marriage

Marriage is good for the nation. When a marriage succeeds, the nation succeeds. Strong marriages, including yours, are good for EVERYONE! Neighborhoods, churches, schools, businesses, industry, law enforcement, unions, city government, fire and rescue personnel, and even the state legislature all are winners when marriages succeed.

Marriage is the real "jackpot" in life in which everyone from every segment of society benefits. But men are the biggest winners when marriage succeeds. Research shows that when men are successful in marriage they become better men.[3]

Consider this: when most women have a child, at whatever age, they begin to mature and consider the child's needs before their own. This seems to be true for teens who become single moms as well as for adult women who are married. Certainly there are women who do not care for their children, but as a pattern, women do not abandon their children even during difficult times. However, the same is not true for men. When men father children, they do not necessarily mature and become better men. In fact, there are entire communities in which the father is usually absent from the family because he is not mature enough to take on the responsibilities of being a dad.[4]

What causes a man to mature, especially in his interpersonal life? Research shows that it is a committed relationship to a woman! Yes, men do mature through responsibility; but for most men, it is a committed relationship to a woman, usually in marriage, that causes them to think of the needs of someone else before their own.

I, Robert, am a good example of how marriage, not fatherhood, demanded that I grow up. When we started having children I was slow to understand that these children were, well… mine. No, I was not out chasing other women, going to the bars, or playing with my toys (although that is often the case for many men who are fathers). I just took advantage of being able to come and go, assuming that Lori would care for her… I mean, *our* children. One day when I generously offered to baby-sit the children so she could do some kind of self-care activity like… sleep, (no, probably going out with friends), she walked directly up to me. She stared me down, eye-to-eye, with a determined look on her face and said firmly,

"YOU DO NOT BABY-SIT YOUR OWN CHILDREN!"

It was my relationship with Lori that demanded that I grow up and start thinking of the children and her before me.

When this happens to men, when they start placing the needs of their spouses and children before their own as marriage demands, they start receiving the enormous benefits that come from committed love. Research shows that married men have better physical and emotional health and live longer than their single counterparts. Living as a single adult is difficult for most men. Again, research shows that single men drink excessively, engage in unwise and risky behavior, and are more prone to do drugs, and die younger than their married counterparts.[5]

Why are married men healthier, happier, and living longer than their single counter parts? Their wives get them to the doctor, help them to exercise and eat right, and provide them with a satisfying sex life. Yes, married men report happier sex lives than their single, divorced, and widowed counterparts; more on this in Chapter 9.[6]

What are other benefits of marriage for both sexes?

Married couples have greater wealth than their single counterparts. They work together to build wealth as they buy a home, start a retirement plan, and save for their children's college funds.[7]

Married men and women are great neighbors and citizens. When a couple marries, they become clairvoyant; they can see into the future. They can envision raising kids and can even picture grandkids. They want safe neighborhoods with high quality schools, so they get involved with neighborhood committees and school boards. They want their children to have a strong spiritual and moral foundation so they participate in a church.

And if where they live does not offer the kind of life they want their children and grandchildren to have, they move to where they can get it. When my great-grandparents decided to bring their families to America from Sicily, they did not just come for themselves; they came for me and all of my brothers and cousins. They wanted to give us a future better than the present they were living, a future that was safe, prosperous, Catholic, and filled with opportunity. Their success in marriage and in establishing themselves in southern Louisiana laid the foundation for the success of their descendants two generations later.

This does not mean that singles, co-habiting, and divorced people cannot be wealth-builders and good citizens. It does mean that marriage changes a person's perspective on life and influences his or her choices to be, more often than not, a benefit to the rest of society. Take for example a young friend who was single and working as a "travel nurse" in different parts of the country. One year, she worked from January through March in Salt Lake City so she could ski. She took April off to back-pack in Utah, did a medical mission trip in Guatemala, and attended the New Orleans Jazz Festival. She worked from May until the end of September, and then took October off so she could go to Norway with her grandmother and then to Spain with her sister. This really good person was not saving money, she was spending it. And even though she was a great asset wherever she worked, she was not getting involved in her community. There was no need pulling her to get involved.

Studies show that marriage is good for business and corporate America. People who are in successful marriages show up at work on time, are more focused and productive while at work, and take less time off for sickness and health-related issues than their single, co-habiting, divorced, and widowed counterparts. The reverse is also true. Couples who are in relationships that are spiraling out of control are less able to focus at work, often drain their supervisors and co-workers of their energy, and take more time off to manage the fallout of their failing relationships.[8]

And certainly, women are "winners" in successful marriages, for similar reasons that their husbands are "winners." They, too, have greater wealth, health, emotional stability, and better sex lives than their single and cohabiting counterparts — with this added bonus: peace of mind knowing <u>their children have a father who loves her and them</u>.

CHILDREN WIN WHEN MARRIAGES SUCCEED! Studies show that children from intact marriages out-perform children from single parent homes in all academic disciplines. They show greater emotional health and maturity, and, in their adult life, they demonstrate a greater degree of success in their chosen work or professions. The greatest gift that couples <u>can give their children is a home where Mom and Dad love one another</u>. This is better than a college education, music lessons, and Nintendo. **Academic, athletic, and artistic successes, as important as these are, are not what build self-esteem in children. It is being raised in a home where Mom and Dad love one another.**[9]

It is impossible to buy this kind of marriage! No amount of money, political success, physical beauty, or musical talent will obtain for you a successful marriage; otherwise John F. Kennedy and Marilyn Monroe would be our marriage heroes.

This does <u>not</u> mean that single parents cannot be great parents and that single adults cannot be successful in life. It does mean that <u>marriage matters!</u>

The Amazing Gift of Your Marriage Your marriage is a <u>gift</u> to each other, to your children, family and friends, and to the church and society. But how? Waite and Gallagher have identified twelve unique benefits that couples gain when they succeed in marriage. These are:

1. **Teamwork:** Successful couples learn to work together.
2. **Self-Discovery:** Successful couples discover their unique gifts and use them for the good of the family.
3. **Maturity:** Successful couples hold one another accountable; each becomes a better person.
4. **Wealth-Building:** Successful couples take steps to create wealth that will serve the family.
5. **Healthy Lifestyles:** Successful couples eat a balanced diet, exercise, and get enough sleep.
6. **Workplace Success:** Successful couples succeed in the workplace, and for those who are homemakers, in managing the home.
7. **Good Neighbors:** Successful couples get involved in the community.
8. **The Best Caregivers:** Successful couples take care of one another during illness.
9. **Friends:** Successful couples have fun together as life-long friends and companions.
10. **Successful Children:** Successful couples provide the optimum environment within their relationship for their children to succeed.
11. **Mental and Emotional Health:** Successful couples manage stress, learn to work through conflict, and keep a positive view of life.
12. **Great Sex:** Successful couples enjoy a mutually satisfying sex life that is pleasurable, frequent enough, and means, "I love you."[10]

Couple Exercise *How is your marriage a gift? Take the Marriage Assessment and find out. Complete it separately, and then compare your answers. Remember: When your answers do not match up, invite one another to explain. Your goal is to **listen** to one another simply for understanding, not to defend yourself, win an argument, or problem-solve.*

So when you share your responses with one another, use the following communication method to help you become outstanding listeners with one another:

MY TURN / YOUR TURN

1. When it is My Turn to speak, you listen.

2. I will speak in short phrases; you paraphrase what you hear me say.

3. You can invite me to say more or to help you understand something, but you cannot give me your opinion, defend yourself, or try to solve a problem.

4. When I think I have been heard, it will be YOUR TURN to speak, following the same rules.

5. After we have both listened to one another and each has said all that needs to be said, we will work on problem-solving.

Remember, the goal is <u>not</u> to win your spouse to your viewpoint but simply to understand one another.

Marriage Success - An Assessment: (Circle one answer from the multiple choice options.)

Teamwork

1 A.   We work together as a team.
    1) always   2) often   3) sometimes   4) never

1 B   We know how to tackle a project together and successfully complete it.
    1) always   2) often   3) sometimes   4) never

A good memory that I have of our learning to work as a team is...

Self-Discovery

2 A.   My spouse is very gifted and uses his/her gifts to enrich our family.
    1) always   2) often   3) sometimes   4) never

2 B.   My spouse is very aware of my gifts and encourages me to use them to enrich our family.
    1) always   2) often   3) sometimes   4) never

A good memory that I have of each of us using our gifts for the good of the family is...

Maturity

3 A.   Marriage brings out the best in me.
    1) always   2) often   3) sometimes   4) never

3 B.   I can look back on my marriage and see how through it I have become a better person.
    1) always   2) often   3) sometimes   4) never

A good memory that I have of our marriage helping me grow as a person is...

Wealth-Building

4 A.   I am satisfied that we have the money we need to live the lifestyle we want to live.
    1) always   2) often   3) sometimes   4) never

4 B. We agree on our approach to money, how we are to save, spend, and give a portion of it to charity.
    1) always   2) often   3) sometimes   4) never

A good memory that I have when we made a good choice related to money is...

Healthy Lifestyles

5 A.   We are committed to and work at living a healthy lifestyle, including nurturing a spiritual life.
    1) always   2) often   3) sometimes   4) never

5 B.   We have a healthy balance of work, leisure time, diet, exercise, spirituality, and sleep.
        1) always   2) often   3) sometimes   4) never

A good memory that I have of our living a balanced life is...

Workplace Success

6 A.   My relationships at work (or home for the homemaker) are very positive and productive.
        1) always   2) often   3) sometimes   4) never

6 B.   I am confident at what I do and receive affirmation and encouragement for it.
        1) always   2) often   3) sometimes   4) never

A good memory that I have when I truly enjoyed my work and/or being the homemaker is....

Best Caregiver

7 A.   My spouse takes good care of me when I am not feeling well.
        1) always   2) often   3) sometimes   4) never

7 B.   My spouse is the first person that I turn to for care when I am not feeling well.
        1) always   2) often   3) sometimes   4) never

A good memory that I have of my spouse caring for me when I was not feeling well is...

Good Neighbors

8 A.   It is very important to us to be a good neighbor and pay attention to what is going on in the community.
        1) always   2) often   3) sometimes   4) never

8 B.   We are active in helping our neighborhood and community become a better place to live.
        1) always   2) often   3) sometimes   4) never

A good memory that I have of our family reaching out to neighbors is...

Friends

9 A.   My spouse and I are the best of friends; I can fully be myself with my spouse.
        1) always   2) often   3) sometimes   4) never

9 B.   We regularly make time for fun and leisure.
        1) always   2) often   3) sometimes   4) never

A good memory that I have of our being friends is...

FOR THOSE WITH CHILDREN

10 A.   Our children wonderfully enrich our marriage.
      1) always   2) often   3) sometimes   4) never

10 B.   Being parents has brought my spouse and me closer together.
      1) always   2) often   3) sometimes   4) never

A good memory that I have of our being with our children is...

Mental Health

11 A.   We are very good at dealing with conflict.
      1) always   2) often   3) sometimes   4) never

11 B.   We are careful not to hurt one another with our words or actions during a conflict.
      1) always   2) often   3) sometimes   4) never

A good memory that I have of our effectively dealing with a serious problem is...

Great Sex

12 A.   I am satisfied with our sexual life and find it pleasurable, meaningful, and frequent enough.
      1) always   2) often   3) sometimes   4) never

    B.   As we get older we are able to speak with each other about our changing needs related to sex.
      1) always   2) often   3) sometimes   4) never

A good memory that I have of a very satisfying sexual encounter with my spouse is...

Tally your score. Count the number of 1's, 2's, 3's, and 4's you circled. Write down each tally, then multiply that number by the indicated factor (e.g. If you had eight 1's, the score would be 8 x 1 = 8. If you had eight 2's, the score would be 8 x 2 =16, etc.). Add the sums together to determine your total score. **The lower the score, the more successful the marriage**.

With children:
24 to 37 = Very Successful Marriage;
38 to 61 = Successful Marriage;
62 to 86 = Marriage Needs Attention;
87 or greater = HELP!

Without children:
22 to 33 = Very Successful Marriage;
34 to 55 = Successful Marriage;
56 to 76 = Marriage Needs Attention;
77 or greater = HELP!

Example:

Number of 1's: 5 x 1 = 5
Number of 2's: 12 x 2 = 24
Number of 3's: 5 x 3 = 15
Number of 4's: 4 x 1 = 4
Total = 48

Your score:

Number of 1's: _____ x 1 = _____
Number of 2's: _____ x 2 = _____
Number of 3's: _____ x 3 = _____
Number of 4's: _____ x 4 = _____

Total = _____

Reflection Questions:

1. List all the categories where you gave yourself 1's or 2's.

2. List all the categories where you gave yourself 3's or 4's.

3. When I consider the results of the above assessment, I feel _____ because…

4. Some things that I need to do to make our marriage stronger are…

5. Some things that I need from my spouse to make our marriage stronger are…

CHAPTER 3

The Struggle of Marriage in America

Succeeding in marriage in the 21st century is quite a challenge. About half of all first-time marriages end in divorce. Second marriages fail at a higher rate with 67% not making it to "death do us part." [11] Furthermore, many couples are choosing not to marry unless they can first "test the waters." As a young friend told me when he and his girlfriend moved in together, *"She does not want to be divorced like her parents!"*

Why? Why is it such a struggle to be married in America today? The story of Murphy the Marriage Salesman will give us some clues.

Murphy the Marriage Salesman

Murphy the Marriage Salesman sold marriages. He sold marriages of all sorts and sizes with a variety of different perks, privileges, and responsibilities. As he traveled from village to village, he rang a bell and shouted, "Marriage for sale! Marriage for sale! Celebrity Marriages! Political Marriages! Marriages of Convenience and Sacrificial Marriages! Get your marriage license right here."

Senator came up to him and said, "I'll have one of those...let's see. What's a Political Marriage cost?" Murphy said, "Well, initially $5 million dollars."

"Humph. Do I have to be faithful?"

"Nope!"

"Will it help me get elected?"

"Of course! You will marry a gorgeous woman who will give you beautiful children, and the public will think you are the model family. But I warn you, there are lots of hidden costs."

Senator frowned, "Hidden costs, what do mean?"

"Well, your wife is going to demand a hefty sum from year to year to keep up the façade. Then there are the payouts to the other girls, the hush money to your security people and... well... you will have to spend some time with your wife, who won't like you."

Senator said, without hesitation, "I'll take it."

He wrote out a check for $5 million dollars and scurried off to claim his wife.

Murphy continued, "Marriage for sale! Marriage for..." He was interrupted by Actress, a gorgeous blond.

"I want to get married, but I need something that will keep me in the limelight. I love the attention of an adoring public."

"Let's see, you need a Celebrity Marriage."

"Oh good," said Actress. "What's that?"

Murphy pulled out the Celebrity Marriage License and read: "A Celebrity Marriage is a social contract between two people, each who are totally self-absorbed. They marry to gain more public attention together than they could each get separately. They will have children only to further increase the love and attention of an adoring public. The paparazzi will follow their every move; rich people will pay them to attend their parties; and when they divorce, each will sell his or her sad story to the tabloids for millions."

"What's it cost?" demanded Actress.

"The upfront costs for rings, wedding, and honeymoon are paid by your husband and the tabloids. But after that you will have to pay millions for on-going therapy, anti-depressants, drugs and alcohol.

Your public will love you, but you will be a personal wreck."

"I'll take it!" said Actress, as she grabbed the Celebrity Marriage license out of Murphy's hands, and ran off to find a celebrity husband.

21st-Century Male and Female were watching all this and saw a marriage license in Murphy's bag wrapped in gold-leafed ribbon. They said, "Hey, you're hiding something from us. What's this marriage license?"

"Well," said Murphy, "That product is special."

"What's the cost, an arm and a leg?" quipped 21st-Century Male. "Or maybe a rib!" said 21st-Century Female.

She continued, "We're on the fast track to the American dream! We've got looks, talent, and an endless line of credit."

He joined in, "We've been living together for a year now; we know all we need to know about life together. What sort of marriage could be better than this?"

Murphy looked at this confident young couple and said, "Well, in this special package is our most unique marriage. It's the only license that will give you a happy marriage."

"Ha! Ha! Ha! You're nuts. There's no such thing as a "Happy Marriage." How much does it cost?"

"Not much, the upfront cost is only $50. But, you will be happy!"

"$50 bucks and we'll be happy? C'mon."

"Really and truly. I'm not saying that you will be happy every minute of every day, but the overall pattern of your life will be love, joy, peace, patience, kindness, generosity, faithfulness, gentleness, self-control, and... a satisfying sex life."

The couple burst into laughter.

"What a charade! Fifty bucks couldn't buy happiness, and it certainly can't give you a satisfying sex life."

"True," said Murphy, "money can't buy happiness, but a Sacrificial Marriage can bring you happiness. That's what this marriage license is for, a Sacrificial Marriage."

"The $50 is the upfront cost; it's for the rings. The price of the Sacrificial Marriage is YOU! You must, without reservation, give yourselves to one another. No HOLDING BACK!"

"OUCH!"

"Furthermore, you're in it for life."

"For Life? OUCH!"

"And lastly you both agree to welcome children."

"Yikes! This is crazy!"

"Yes, it is demanding, but not impossible. You see, you and your partner make three vows to one another. You vow to be faithful in good times and in bad, in sickness and in health, and to love and honor one another until death do you part."

"I don't know," said 21st-Century Male. "What about a license for something easier, something more temporary?"

"That's the license for a Marriage of Convenience. The upfront cost for it is also $50. It has the outward look of the Sacrificial Marriage license, but after seven years you renegotiate to stay together, but live independent lives."

"You forget about fidelity, love, and honor, and when the kids graduate from high school, you realize that you are strangers and divorce. That's where the added costs come in. The divorce will be messy and each of you will have to hire..."

"We'll take it."

Murphy continued. *"Marriage for sale. Marriage for sale!"*

Think about it: What's the story about?

What do the different marriage licenses for sale — the political marriage, celebrity marriage, marriage of convenience, and sacrificial marriage — say about marriage in American society?

Marriage in America is up for grabs. People make it whatever they want it to be to help them pursue the life they want to live. Marriage ought to provide the healthy boundaries of a couple's relationship and shape their commitment to one another. The reverse happens in American culture. Marriage is easily manipulated for personal gain, and sometimes couples are not really aware of how they are shaping marriage by their self-centeredness rather than allowing marriage to draw them together in unity.

Our Story as told by Lori

We bought the "sacrificial marriage" license, but it could have morphed into the marriage of convenience.

In 1984, we were living in South Louisiana where Rob was working in youth ministry and I was a stay-at-home mom with three babies. It became clear to us that if Rob was going to make a career of ministry he needed some credentials and extra training, so off we moved to Maryland where he could go to graduate school at the Washington Theological Union and Catholic University.

Rob, of course, had to keep working full-time in youth ministry, which meant late nights and weekends, and I continued to be a stay-at-home, "natural-family-planning" mom, now with four and then five children. Our lives diverged in different directions: my life was filled with elementary school, pre-school, after-school commitments, babies,

and housework; his with early morning classes; afternoon, evening and weekend work; and studying during his free time.

We both soon became OVERWORKED, OVERTIRED, AND UNDER AVAILABLE TO ONE ANOTHER. I felt like a single mom from September to May, and the kids felt it too. Four-year-old Clare once told her dad, "You ought to play with your wife and kids sometime."

My needs weren't being met – help with the diapers, dishes, and car-pooling, and the absence of adult contact and conversation. Rob's needs weren't being met – fun with the family, romance, and... romance, and...

Oh, he tried to soften the blow with occasional flowers, dinner out and a movie, and late-night rendezvous (which were hard because I was a zombie past 10:00 p.m.). I was guilt-ridden with the growing resentment I felt towards him. He was doing so much good for others and studying so hard, but enough already!

I finally told Rob that I was committed to our marriage (that sacrificial marriage), but was feeling pretty numb in the relationship. I did not need flowers, a date, romance, etc., I needed him home! PERIOD!

That was a turning point for us. We learned that even though we had signed up for the sacrificial marriage, we could easily become roommates in a relationship of convenience if we were not intentional about our marriage. We also learned how poorly we communicated with one another, that our skills at listening and talking to each other, especially around our personal needs, were pathetic.

One day, we decided to write down what we needed from one another. I wrote down that

I needed someone to do what he said he would do in a timely manner, do the work around the house without asking about what needed to be done, be on time, leave early for events, and pay attention to detail.

Rob said he needed someone who didn't stress about the details of life, was spontaneous, went with the flow, and valued relationships over organization.

When we showed each other our lists we laughed! I had described me and Rob had described himself. We did not want to be married to each other. We wanted to be married to ourselves. (But what a nightmare that would be!) The good qualities that we had found so attractive in each other had now grown old and tiresome.

But the lesson of all this became very clear: we had not fully accepted one another. It was time to start over with our sacrificial marriage by fully accepting one another with all the gifts and limitations each possessed.

There were other lessons. We learned that, in spite of our lofty commitment to this sacrificial marriage, we were as vulnerable to the temptations of the world as any other couple. And our temptations were not for the obvious marriage-busting allurements – money, drugs, alcohol, material possessions, or another person.

Our ambitions were cloaked in religion, which made it harder for us to see their negative impact on our marriage. But they were just as real: ministry to youth with no time boundaries, living simply on a ministry salary while having a big family, fully participating in parish and community life while raising this large family, working full-time while attending graduate school. The center of Rob's life was not me, nor the children, but his studies and work. The center of my life was not Rob; it was the children and their demanding schedules of school, sports, music lessons, and religious education. We were both wrong not to give our marriage a higher priority.

Never again would we let our marriage slip into a marriage of convenience. We renewed our commitment to work on our marriage every day, and our marriage has worked. It is not a perfect marriage, but it is a successful and happy one that includes six children: Steven, Clare, Mary, Kate, Andrew, and Colleen.

Couple Exercise: *What is something in our story that resonates with your story? Why did you get married? Take the following assessment and find out.*

Why I Married: An Assessment — *Indicate your agreement with each statement by circling one of the four words beneath each statement that most corresponds to why you married. Complete separately and compare your answers. Use My Turn/Your Turn as needed.*

1. My fiancé had good connections, and I thought this marriage would help me get ahead in life.
   Absolutely   Somewhat   Not Really   No

2. My fiancé had money and a knack for making money, and together we could live a lifestyle that would require large incomes.
   Absolutely   Somewhat   Not Really   No

3. Marriage was the ticket out of my home and family, which was not a good place to be.
   Absolutely   Somewhat   Not Really   No

4. We sort of slipped into marriage after realizing we liked being together.
   Absolutely   Somewhat   Not Really   No

5. I was passionately in love, and marriage seemed to be the logical next step.
   Absolutely   Somewhat   Not Really   No

6. I knew that this was the person that I wanted to be the other parent of my children.
   Absolutely   Somewhat   Not Really   No

7. The sex was great. Why not get married?
   Absolutely   Somewhat   Not Really   No

8. Our friends were all getting married, and it seemed like a good idea for us to do so.
   Absolutely   Somewhat   Not Really   No

9. I felt pressure from my family to find a suitable spouse who had career goals and was attractive.
   Absolutely   Somewhat   Not Really   No

10. We both sensed that God was calling us to marriage, and we could not wait to have kids.
    Absolutely   Somewhat   Not Really   No

11. Is there a reason that you married that is not part of this list? If so, what is it?

CHAPTER 4

Taming the Tongue

The old saying from grade school, *"Sticks and stones may break my bones but words will never hurt me,"* is a lie. We all know that negative words can hurt mightily. And we live in a culture of late night comedians and radio talk shows that thrive on sarcasm and one-liners that zing stones against public figures and against callers phoning in who may have a different point of view. This is an age- old problem, as the following New Testament reading from the letter of James (1:26, 3:3-10) illustrates:

If anyone thinks he is religious and does not bridle his tongue but deceives his heart, his religion is vain... If we put bits into the mouths of horses to make them obey us, we also guide their whole bodies.

It is the same with ships: even though they are so large and driven by fierce winds, they are steered by a very small rudder wherever the pilot's inclination wishes.

In the same way the tongue is a small member and yet has great pretensions. Consider how small a fire can set a huge forest ablaze. It exists among our members as a world of malice, defiling the whole body and setting the entire course of our lives on fire...

For every kind of beast and bird, of reptile and sea creature, can be tamed and has been tamed by the human species, but no human being can tame the tongue.

It is a restless evil, full of deadly poison. With it we bless the Lord and Father, and with it we curse human beings who are made in the image of God.

From the same mouth come blessing and curse. This need not be so, my brothers [and sisters].

These are difficult words to hear. Rob does not have a wicked tongue. His temptation is not to hurt people with his words, but to withdraw in silence, tell a joke, or make up some kind of idiotic story to get a laugh, but avoid dealing with the issue at hand.

But I, Lori, I'm a word pro. I grew up reading the dictionary. I listen to Will Short, the "Puzzle Master," every Sunday morning on NPR. Scrabble is my game of choice, and it's an adrenalin rush to attack the daily crossword puzzle. I'm good with words when trying to describe my thoughts and feelings on paper. And, I'm ashamed to say, I can be very sarcastic when I'm tired, feel disregarded or, worse, attacked. (May my children forgive me!)

When our needs are not being met, needs like affection, conversation, sexual fulfillment, financial stability, parenting and domestic support, fun and recreational companionship, respect and admiration, trust and friendship, we tend to do one or another of the following: FIGHT, FLIGHT, OR STINKING THINKING.

Fight – You or your spouse feels defensive about a comment. You know the best defense is an offense, so you go on the attack. This might look like a louder voice, a finger poke in the chest, or intensifying the debate. When this happens, someone has stopped listening, and you need to call, "Time-out!"

Flight – You or your spouse feels hurt by a comment. You can fight it out, but why bother? You withdraw by being quiet, telling a joke, or actually leaving. When this happens, someone has stopped listening, and you need to call, "Time-out!"

Stinking Thinking – You or your spouse does not understand what the other is trying to say. But you've lived with her/him for a long time and you can fill in the story with all the negative interpretations that your creative mind can conjure up. When this happens, someone has stopped listening, and you need to call, "Time-out!"

Time Out [12] Call "Time-out" anytime you detect that "fight, flight, and stinking thinking" are rearing their ugly heads. These are the warning signs that <u>someone is not listening.</u>

Take a break.

Do something that is relaxing and refreshing, and then come back together to continue your discussion, but be sure to come back together to talk. "Time-out" without "time-in" is another word for "Flight!"

When you do call "time-in," use *My Turn/Your Turn* to help you listen to one another. Flip a coin to see who goes first.

MY TURN/YOUR TURN

1. When it is MY TURN I speak, you listen.

2. I will speak in short phrases; you paraphrase what you hear me say.

3. You can invite me to say more or to help you understand something, but you cannot give me your opinion, defend yourself, or try to solve a problem.

4. When I think I have been heard, it will be YOUR TURN to speak following the same rules.

5. After we have both listened to one another and each has said all that he or she needs to say, we will work on problem-solving.

When "*fight, flight, and stinking thinking*" are lurking around, couples are at high risk for hurting one another. They usually do this with one or more of what we call the "Dirty Dozen." These are the twelve fundamental negative ways of miscommunication that couples use when they respond from hurt, fear, or anger.

Once spoken, the Dirty Dozen do their damage and are terribly difficult to undo. Think about it. Your boss yells at you for missing an assignment.

"YOU NO GOOD, LAZY, GOOD-FOR-NOTHING BLANKETY BLANK!"

How many positive words is it going to take from him (or her) to help restore your confidence? What if the words come from someone much closer, perhaps from your father or spouse? How deeply do those words wound? How many positive words and affirmations does it take to undo the damage of those comments? The answer is, of course, very, very many!

Here are the "Dirty Dozen" ways of Negative Communication. [13] When any of these methods for dealing with unmet needs are present, it is certain that someone is not listening.

Solution Messages: I know better than you.

1. Telling the other person what to do.

2. Warning or even threatening the other with consequences.

3. Moralizing. You should or ought to do this. Persuasion through guilt!

4. Advising and problem-solving. Message: I'm smart; you're dumb.

5. Persuading with logic and lecturing: trying to influence the other person with facts.

6. Probing and questioning: digging for answers

7. Analyzing and diagnosing: figuring out motives.

Put Down Messages: "There's something wrong with you that needs to change."

8. Criticizing and blaming.

9. Name-calling, ridiculing, and using sarcasm.

Denial Messages: "I do not want to know how you are feeling."

10. Praise and approval. Manipulating through flattery.

11. Reassuring and consoling. (When done too soon, it minimizes the other's feelings.)

12. Withdrawing, distracting, or using humor.

Couple exercise: *Do the "Power of Words Inventory" to help you identify which of the "Dirty Dozen" your spouse is most likely to use against you. Share your answers using My Turn/Your Turn as needed. Keep in mind there may be an appropriate time for most of these communication strategies, but not when you need to listen. For example, my wife comes home from school complaining about her day, and I interrupt her with "Lori, you are a great teacher and that school is lucky to have you." What I have actually done is use a compliment to cut her off and not listen to her bad day at school. She may need a compliment, but now is not the time. What she needs is for me to say, "Tell me about your day."*

Power of Words Inventory On a scale from 1 to 10 indicate your level of agreement with the following statements with a 10 = Yes, 5 = Sometimes, and a 1 = No.

	No				Sometimes					Yes
1. My spouse orders me around and tells me what to do.	1	2	3	4	5	6	7	8	9	10
2. My spouse threatens me with consequences.	1	2	3	4	5	6	7	8	9	10
3. My spouse tells me what I should and should not do, and tries to persuade me through guilt.	1	2	3	4	5	6	7	8	9	10
4. My spouse gives me solutions and advice when I try to talk to him/her.	1	2	3	4	5	6	7	8	9	10
5. My spouse lectures and tries to persuade me with facts and figures.	1	2	3	4	5	6	7	8	9	10
6. My spouse interrogates and digs for information.	1	2	3	4	5	6	7	8	9	10
7. My spouse analyzes my motives and behaviors and has figured out what I think before I do.	1	2	3	4	5	6	7	8	9	10
8. My spouse criticizes, judges, and blames.	1	2	3	4	5	6	7	8	9	10
9. My spouse ridicules, calls me names, and uses sarcasm.	1	2	3	4	5	6	7	8	9	10
10. My spouse manipulates by saying what I want to hear, but does not tell me the full truth.	1	2	3	4	5	6	7	8	9	10
11. My spouse disregards my feelings and emotions through humor and jokes.	1	2	3	4	5	6	7	8	9	10
12. My spouse withdraws through silence and/or busyness.	1	2	3	4	5	6	7	8	9	10

Reflection Questions:

1. When my spouse speaks to me using any of the above negative ways of communication I feel _____ _____ because...

2. When I look at the above list, I am guilty of doing numbers...

When personal needs are not being met Now you might ask, "If I cannot do any of these responses while listening to my spouse, what can I do?" The answer is, "Listen." Some of these responses may eventually be appropriate, but when used too early they cut off the speaker and keep you from listening. This includes praising, reassuring, and offering consolation and support.

We have little control over our gut reactions and emotions in response to our spouse's problematic behavior and our unmet needs. But we are still responsible for what we do in response to our reactions and emotions. Psychology teaches us that emotions are neutral, neither good nor bad. They come with life. What we do with them, such as anger, is what's important. St. Paul confirms this when he writes:

"Be angry but do not sin; do not let the sun set on your anger, and do not leave room for the devil… No foul language should come out of your mouths, but only such as is good for needed edification, that it may impart grace to those who hear." (Ephesians 4:26-29)

We like the line, "Be angry but do not sin." Here is how we learned to acknowledge our emotions and gut reactions without hurting our spouse with any of the "Dirty Dozen."

Our Story by Lori Rob and I learned early on that we were very different from one another, and that was not going to change. So, if our needs were not being met in the relationship we needed to communicate clearly, and avoid using our favorite versions of the "Dirty Dozen." We needed to learn to be angry, sad, discouraged, whatever, and communicate that to each other without hurting or sinning against one another. We had to learn how to send one another a straight message by using an X, Y, Z Statement:

When you do _____ X (name the behavior)

I feel _____ Y (name the feelings that surface with the behavior)

because _____ Z (try to explain why the behavior named is a problem for you).[14]

Rob and I had to practice giving one another straight messages before it became natural. But because they worked and helped us clarify misunderstandings while protecting our relationship, we kept working at them. For example, one day while we were driving the back streets of Seattle, where there are numerous unmarked intersections, I was a bit unrelenting in giving Rob driving instructions.

When we arrived at our home, Rob, who was obviously perturbed with me, decided he would send me a "Straight Message:"

Lori, when you tell me how to drive over and over again… (X, the problematic behavior)

I feel irritated… (Y, the feelings evoked by X)

because I've been driving safely for over 30 years and know how to drive. I'm not a child that needs a driving instructor (Z, explanation why X is a problem).

He did a good job in naming my nagging behavior without attacking me. So I sent him a straight message back:

Rob, when you do not slow down at unmarked intersections… (X, the problematic behavior)

I feel scared… (Y, feelings evoked by X)

because I'm afraid we are going to get in a wreck (Z, explanation why X is a problem).

This was an "A-ha Moment" for both of us. It never occurred to Rob that I was afraid *of me or the kids getting hurt if he got in a wreck. He apparently thought I was nagging him because I like to nag. He said, "Oh, my goodness, I'm sorry. I don't want you to be afraid while I'm driving. I can slow down at the unmarked intersections."*

You have probably guessed that this is an on-going challenge for us. I try to trust his driving, and he tries to be patient with my "instructions" about driving. Sometimes we still have to communicate clearly when I am nervous about his driving, and he is bothered by my giving him driving directions, but we never make it personal. We focus on the behavior.

Learning how to send a "Straight Message" is essential in breaking the habit of the "Dirty Dozen." A "Straight Message" deals with behavior and does not attack the person doing the behavior. When delivering a "Straight Message," it is most important that you use non-judgmental words to describe the problematic behavior. Remember, you are trying to protect the relationship, not add fuel to the fire.

The power of a "Straight Message" is that it helps you to mirror back to your spouse how his or her behavior is impacting you. You cannot change your spouse's behavior, but by telling your spouse in a clear non-judgmental way that his or her behavior is a problem for you, you place the responsibility to change behavior on your spouse. You do not have to yell, scream, shout, pout, or withdraw to communicate clearly to your spouse that his or her behavior is a problem for you. Send a straight message; if your spouse continues the problematic behavior, then you have a choice to change your behavior.

Practice sending each other a "Straight Message."
The X, Y, Z Statement works with sending compliments as well as dealing with difficult topics. Each couple takes a turn practicing sending an X, Y, Z statement. The listener listens using My Turn/Your Turn.

1. When I think of my childhood (X), I feel (Y)_____because (Z)...

2. When I receive a compliment from my boss (X), I feel (Y)_____ because (Z) ...

3. When I think about current national affairs (X), I feel (Y)_____ because (Z)...

4. When my spouse remembers my birthday (X), I feel (Y)_____ because (Z)...

5. When I think about Christmas (X), I feel (Y) _____ because (Z)...

6. When you did (X)_____ (something positive your spouse did), I felt (Y) _____ because (Z)...

7. When you did (X)_____ (another positive your spouse did), I felt (Y) _____ because (Z)...

8. When you did (X)_____ (name a negative behavior), I felt (Y) _____ because (Z)...

9. When you did (X) _____ (another negative behavior), I felt (Y) _____ because (Z)...

CHAPTER 5

Marriage Wisdom from Catholics

We wrote in the introduction that this book is for anyone who wants to succeed in marriage, not just Catholics — even though we are drawing on the Catholic vision for marriage as our roadmap to a healthy marriage. We are convinced that the Catholic vision for marriage is universal. It is for everyone, across cultures and creeds.

The best place to look for the Catholic view on marriage is the Marriage Rite. In the Catholic wedding, just before the couple exchanges vows, they are asked to state their intentions.

Have you come here freely and without reservation to give yourselves to each other in marriage?

Will you love and honor each other as husband and wife for the rest of your lives?

Will you accept children lovingly from God, and bring them up according to the law of Christ and his Church?

A marriage is a life-long covenant between a woman and man, freely entered, and open to the possibility of life. In fact, if your teenager asks you when is it okay for him or her to have sex, you can say, "When you and your love interest are prepared to give yourself to one another, without reservation, in a life-long covenant that is open to having children, you are ready for sex; therefore, get married."

Now let's look at each of these questions more closely, and after we do, you will have a relationship assessment related to these questions to complete with your spouse.

Have you come here freely and without reservation to give yourselves to each other in marriage?

For a marriage to be valid, the motivation for it cannot be political – an arranged relationship to give one or the other spouse, or both, social leverage.

It cannot be coerced. Shotgun weddings, for whatever reason, are not valid. Marriage must be freely entered without any impairment, e.g. one cannot be drunk or stoned on the wedding day, as a buddy of mine was (and so was his best man). This makes a "free decision" impossible.

Nor can a spouse answer "yes" to the question, but really mean "no." A young friend concluded two weeks before her wedding date, after all the invitations had been mailed, presents were being delivered and out-of-town guests had made their travel arrangements, that she no longer loved her fiancé. When asked this question by the priest at the ceremony, she said, "Yes," but meant "No!"

For a marriage to be valid it must be freely entered without reservation. This does <u>not</u> mean without nervousness and uncertainty about what the future may bring. Of course, couples will be nervous. But their intention is clear: they wish to give of themselves to one another.

Pope John Paul II, in reflecting on the encounter between a man and a woman in sexual intimacy, stated that this very human act implies a nuptial purpose even without referring to religious faith. When two people come together in sexual union, they are not just two bodies having a go for sexual pleasure. They are two persons - each with hopes, dreams, feelings, histories, and desires – who in freedom, without any coercion, offer to one another and receive from the other the gift of self.

I cannot go into all the details of his "Theology of the Body" here. But in summary, John Paul teaches that the "soil" or "ground" which allows this free gift of self to bloom into a beautiful relationship is committed love. "Committed love" is <u>implicit</u> in the very act of sexual intimacy, because the giving of self that happens in sex demands a covenant in order for this sharing of persons to actually happen. (Sex also implies a commitment between partners because in its most elemental form, without any sort of barrier, sexual intimacy begets children, and children need parents who are committed to one another so that they can grow up and flourish in life.)[15]

This "free gift of self" that spouses offer to one another does not stay up in the clouds as some philosophic theory, but gets worked out in very pragmatic ways, by negotiating how they are to meet one another's most basic interpersonal needs. There are a number of excellent books out that make this point. Two that we like are *His Needs, Her Needs* by Dr. William Harley and *The Five Love Languages* by Gary Chapman.

In *His Needs, Her Needs*, William Harley makes the case that those marriages that succeed do so because couples have found a way to negotiate the following fundamental needs (not wants) of a marriage relationship:

1. Parental Involvement
2. Admiration
3. Affection
4. Sexual Fulfillment
5. Domestic Support
6. Financial Support
7. Honesty
8. Attractive Spouse
9. Conversation
10. Recreational Companion

Couple Activity: Harley thinks that husbands and wives have a different priority list. Take a moment for you and your spouse to select the five most important needs for men and the five most important needs for women; then compare your answers. (See endnote 15 for Harley's lists.)[16]

St. Paul understood this, that marriage means negotiating needs. (1 Corinthians 7:3-8)

The husband should fulfill his duty toward his wife, and likewise the wife toward her husband. A wife does not have authority over her own body, but rather her husband, and similarly a husband does not have authority over his own body, but rather

his wife. Do not deprive each other, except perhaps by mutual consent for a time, to be free for prayer, but then return to one another, so that Satan may not tempt you through your lack of self-control.

This I say by way of concession, however, not as a command. Indeed, I wish everyone to be as I am, but each has a particular gift from God, one of one kind and one of another. Now to the unmarried and to widows, I say: it is a good thing for them to remain as they are, as I do, but if they cannot exercise self-control they should marry, for it is better to marry than to be on fire.

In *The Five Love Languages*, Gary Chapman writes about how spouses learn to negotiate needs in a different way. He proposes that most women and men have preferred ways to give and receive love:

1. Physical touch
2. Giving gifts
3. Spending quality time together
4. Speaking kindly
5. Doing acts of service.[17]

However, most people do not understand this and tend to show love to their spouses in the same way that they prefer to be loved. We were guilty of this.

When our kids were young and I, Robert, would come in late at night following an evening of youth ministry, I was ready for some physical touch and kind words, my love language. I easily overlooked the dishes piled to the ceiling in the sink, the mound of diapers to fold on the couch, and the toys scattered across the living room floor.

Lori could not. Doing acts of service is her love language. She is not mentally prepared to be touched or to touch me in an intimate way until the work of the house is done. Life became much easier after we figured this out.

Couple Exercise *Complete the Interpersonal Inventory and Love Language Inventory to help you determine how well you are negotiating meeting your "interpersonal needs" and loving one another as each of you prefers to be loved. Share your answers using My Turn/Your Turn as needed.*

Interpersonal Inventory Spouses have certain interpersonal needs that they agree will be met exclusively through one another. The challenge is to become aware of these needs and communicate them in healthy ways. On a scale from 1-10 indicate your level of agreement with the following statements with a 10 = Yes, 5 = Sometimes, and a 1 = No.

	No				Sometimes					Yes
1. I trust my spouse when he/she is away.	1	2	3	4	5	6	7	8	9	10
2. I make time to talk on a regular basis.	1	2	3	4	5	6	7	8	9	10
3. My spouse listens to me.	1	2	3	4	5	6	7	8	9	10
4. I can be fully myself with my spouse.	1	2	3	4	5	6	7	8	9	10
5. My spouse does not try to change me.	1	2	3	4	5	6	7	8	9	10
6. My spouse is affectionate.	1	2	3	4	5	6	7	8	9	10
7. My spouse is kind.	1	2	3	4	5	6	7	8	9	10
8. I like my spouse's family.	1	2	3	4	5	6	7	8	9	10
9. My spouse acts in my best interest.	1	2	3	4	5	6	7	8	9	10
10. My spouse never takes me for granted.	1	2	3	4	5	6	7	8	9	10
11. My spouse enjoys my friends.	1	2	3	4	5	6	7	8	9	10
12. My spouse understands me better than anyone.	1	2	3	4	5	6	7	8	9	10
13. I feel safe with my spouse.	1	2	3	4	5	6	7	8	9	10
14. My spouse isn't very controlling.	1	2	3	4	5	6	7	8	9	10
15. My spouse shares his/her feelings.	1	2	3	4	5	6	7	8	9	10
16. My spouse shows me lots of appreciation.	1	2	3	4	5	6	7	8	9	10
17. I admire my spouse.	1	2	3	4	5	6	7	8	9	10

When I consider how different we are from each other and the basic needs that I have for trust, friendship, fun, intimacy, acceptance, and appreciation, I feel _____ because…

Something that I think we need to do to better meet one another's interpersonal needs is…

Discovering How I Prefer to Give and Receive Love (See *The Five Love Languages,* by Gary Chapman, for a more thorough exercise to discover your Love Language). There are 10 pairs of sentences below. Each one states how a person likes to be loved and cared for. Compare the sentences in a set and indicate your preference in each pair by marking a check in the space provided. Compile your answers using the chart below.

1 ____I feel so good when you send me flowers. (B)
____I like it when you give me hugs. (A)

2. ____I am grateful when you bring me a new DVD. (B)
____I enjoy playing a board game with you. (C)

3. ____I love it when you say, "Thank you." (D)
____It is fun riding bikes with you. (C)

4. ____I need to hear you speak kindly even on difficult topics. (D)
____I really appreciate it when you prepare a snack for me. (E)

5. ____It is so great to sit next to you and feel your body next to mine. (A)
____I like taking a walk with you. (C)

6. ____A back rub feels really good. (A)
____I appreciate it when you give me a compliment. (D)

7. ____I love to read and enjoy getting a book. (B)
____I am grateful when you do your share of the work around home. (E)

8. ____I like holding hands with you. (A)
____I appreciate it when you run errands for me. (E)

9. ____I get so excited when you give me a music CD. (B)
____I sure like being encouraged by positive words from you. (D)

10. ____I like to have time to sit and be together. (C)
____I am grateful when you help me to succeed at my commitments. (E)

Add up the number of the letters that you selected and place them in the column to the right.	**Totals**
	A___ Touch
	B___ Gifts
	C___ Quality Time
	D___ Kind Words
	E___ Service
	Your Love language is…

Reflection question: I feel most loved by you when you do _____ because…

Will you love and honor each other as husband and wife for the rest of your lives?

The "rest of your lives" can be a long time if you live as long as most Americans are living today. Imagine being married to your spouse for 50-60 years. The key to longevity in marriage is being the best of friends as spouses.

A faithful friend is a sturdy shelter; he who finds one finds a treasure. A faithful friend is beyond price, no sum can balance his worth. A faithful friend is a life-saving remedy, such as he who fears God finds; for he who fears God behaves accordingly, and his friend will be like himself (Sirach 6:14-17)**.**

Our Story, from Lori *Our relationship began when we met at the Catholic campus ministry at Louisiana State University. A mutual friend recruited me to join the outreach to the local nursing home, since I had a car and could drive students, and she recruited Rob because he had a guitar and could lead the entertainment.*

It took me a while to become friends with Rob because he was so LOUD and had such an IMPOSING personality. I was just the opposite - a wallflower, hiding in a corner, not wanting to be noticed. What won me over was his kind, genuine heart, and that he was such a good listener. He was sincerely interested in this quiet, book-oriented young woman, so different from his athletic and spontaneous self. And we began to grow in love and friendship with one another when we discovered we both enjoyed music and riding bikes, and we shared high ideals about faith, children, and serving the poor.

Our Story from Robert *When I think about being friends with Lori over these many years of married life, there is one quality about it that stands out above all the rest: I am basically able to be myself with her, and she is able to be herself with me.*

I say basically because I know that sometimes being myself can be a pain to her, like the time when we met at a dance in college and I dragged her out on the dance floor, and there was no one else there because the band had taken a break, although there was music playing on a boom box. She didn't like that.

Our friendship blossomed quickly, and just eighteen months after meeting, we were married. We loved singing together, riding bikes, and playing board games. But as the children came and grew older, we found that there was a major challenge to our friendship: having fun together. Introverted Lori wanted to spend Sunday mornings going to church and then in bed reading the paper; extroverted Robert wanted to go on a twenty-mile bike ride. Intelligent Lori wanted to do the Crossword Puzzle or play Scrabble. Sports-minded Robert wanted to go to the high school football game or play tennis.

Apparently this is a common issue for couples who, when they were dating, gladly participated in what their love interest enjoyed, but after marriage quietly let that go. We had to learn how to mature together, compromise, and continue to have fun as friends, but accept our differences. I do not do the Crossword Puzzle, but I play Scrabble. Lori will watch college football with me on T.V., and we will walk, bike, and hike for our "sports" activities.

Friendship is the glue that holds together the covenant of marriage. Friendship means you enjoy one another, trust each other implicitly, and feel totally comfortable being yourself when you are together. And, according to researchers, one of the clearest signs of friendship is the capacity for a couple to have fun together. When fun is absent from a marriage it is a good indication that friendship is in trouble.[18] And when friendship is threatened, joy seeps out of the relationship.

Couple Exercise *Complete the Friendship Inventory separately; compare your answers using My Turn/ Your Turn as needed.*

Friendship Inventory On a scale from 1-10 indicate your level of agreement with the following statements with a 10 = Yes, 5 = Sometimes, and a 1 = No.

	No			Sometimes				Yes		
1. We have many common interests.	1	2	3	4	5	6	7	8	9	10
2. I'm okay with the leisure time my spouse spends separate from me.	1	2	3	4	5	6	7	8	9	10
3. We can afford my spouse's leisure activities.	1	2	3	4	5	6	7	8	9	10
4. We often do fun things together.	1	2	3	4	5	6	7	8	9	10
5. My spouse spends too much time with friends.	1	2	3	4	5	6	7	8	9	10
6. My spouse spends too much time with hobbies.	1	2	3	4	5	6	7	8	9	10
7. I tell my spouse everything.	1	2	3	4	5	6	7	8	9	10
8. My spouse tells me everything.	1	2	3	4	5	6	7	8	9	10
9. I trust my spouse to keep intimate matters private.	1	2	3	4	5	6	7	8	9	10
10. I can count on my spouse during difficult times.	1	2	3	4	5	6	7	8	9	10
11. My spouse spends too much time watching T.V.	1	2	3	4	5	6	7	8	9	10
12. My spouse spends too much time with electronic stuff from the cell phone to computer.	1	2	3	4	5	6	7	8	9	10
13. We go on dates on a regular basis.	1	2	3	4	5	6	7	8	9	10
14. I can be myself with my spouse.	1	2	3	4	5	6	7	8	9	10

What are four activities that we do together for fun?
1.
2.
3.
4.
What fun activities do we do separately?
1. He:
2. She:
3. He:
4. She:

When I think about how we relate to one another as Friends, I feel _____ because:

Some things I think we could do to strengthen our friendship are:
1.
2.
3.

Will you accept children lovingly from God, and bring them up according to the law of Christ and his Church?[19]

Why do most women "swish" when they walk? A woman's pelvis and hip bones are made to carry a baby and move from side to side to give the baby the most comfortable ride possible. When I, Robert, was in Haiti and South Africa teaching relationship skills, I could not help but notice the many women carrying large bundles on their heads, but rarely men.

Men can carry heavy loads on their backs, but not their heads. A woman's center of gravity is different from a man's because of her different bone structure involving her hips. This is only one of many physical characteristics of a woman's body that is designed to conceive, carry, birth, and feed a child. But a woman needs a man to conceive a child, and the child needs a marriage of faith, hope, and love to help him or her grow to become a thriving adult.

Sex is not just intended for the giving and receiving of love between spouses, but also for the birthing of children within a covenant of love. In fact, sexual intercourse, without any sort of birth control, clearly implies the possibility of new life and the necessity of commitment between the couple (for their sake and the sake of the children).

Children are a great gift to marriage, but they are work. Children will demand every ounce of Christian commitment and maturity from their parents, and may be the cause of untold tiredness, sacrifice, expenses, and trauma. Children, by their very presence, demand that a mom and dad think and act beyond their own needs to meet the needs of their naturally egocentric, questioning, exploring, whining, pouting, and tantrum-throwing blessings.

Newlyweds and Preparing for Children We do wish we had had more time as a married couple without children. We would have continued doing what we loved doing to strengthen our friendship: take long bike rides, attend retreats, sing together at Mass, read late into the night, and have long evenings for romance. Newlyweds have a wonderful chance to strengthen their marriages before children come and demand so much attention.

Our Story, from Robert We thought that I would be finished with graduate school before we started having children, but that was not to be. Baby One came just two months after I graduated from college; graduate school was put on hold. We thought nothing of it. Welcoming that child into our home and providing for his care took center stage,

BUT I was totally unprepared for it! I did not have a clue what caring for children entailed because, being the sixth of seven boys, I never had to baby-sit. I had never changed a diaper, held an inconsolable infant wanting his mom, or awakened for a middle-of-the-night feeding.

I was on a steep learning curve. Yes, we did the natural birthing classes and I learned to be my wife's coach. We prepared a room in our small apartment for the baby; and Lori gave birth to a fine, strapping boy with the help of a midwife. Then we returned to our home, miles away from either of our mothers, with our precious child. Now what? My goodness, we had to learn to be parents without a trial run.

Our Story, From Lori There are so many joys and wonders in raising children: nursing baby and mom in perfect contentment; baby's first step, word, and tooth; siblings helping their younger sibling to speak – Clare to Mary: "I'm a dirl and you a dirl; daddy's a boy;" — teaching children to read, throw a ball, help with chores; watching Disney movies together and learning all the songs; playing with cousins; doting grandparents; birthday parties; the first day at school; family meals and games; vacations to see family; teaching the children to pray and "participate" in Mass; first signs of teenage-hood, talks on relationships and sexuality; high school sports, drama, art, music, and friends; moving across the country; painting the house; debating bedroom assignments; serving at a *soup kitchen; backyard volleyball and cro-quet, s'mores and singing around the fire-pit.*

And in between all those wondrous moments there were the difficult times: caring for a sick child; arguing over who can do what, when, and with whom; what movie to watch; who gets the bathroom chore this week; who gets to sit in the front seat of the car; what sports can they do this season; refereeing fights, figuring how to pay for music lessons, clothes, a used bike, trips to the county fair, and shirts for the baseball team; and "no you can't go to so-and-so's house unless a parent is there," and "yes, you have to go to Mass as long as you're living in this house."

Newlyweds who understand this can develop positive habits of building a life together that will prepare them for when children come. Natural Family Planning (NFP) can help young couples develop the relationship skills, intimacy, understanding of one another's sexuality and needs, and discipline needed to succeed in marriage. And, of course, NFP will help young couples space the birthing of their children, more or less, as they determine they are prepared to receive them. (And in our ecologically conscious world NFP is totally "a natural." It also is great spiritual discipline – every fast makes the feast so much more celebratory.)

Couples without Children Couples who <u>want</u> children and are <u>unable</u> to have them bear a heavy cross of disappointment and grief. Women especially, when they are young girls, play imaginary games of house and home, picturing themselves as mothers. When this dream is unmet in marriage, it is a great loss of a long-hoped-for future of birthing and caring for children, and can be a grief that they carry throughout their lives. This certainly can also be true for men.

Couples that are unable to have children, for whatever reason, need "something or someone" in their lives, like children, that will draw them

out of themselves in unselfishly giving to others. Children, by their very nature, force parents to grow up. Children demand attention. They must be fed, clothed, bathed, cared for when they are sick, read to, played with, and disciplined. Children truly teach parents to become unselfish and think of their needs and the needs of the family over the individual needs and desires of the parents. This certainly does not happen all the time, but forms a pattern for the lives of the adults.

Couples without children need something like children to teach them to be unselfish, and to help them mature in ways that they simply cannot do on their own. Adoption and/or serving as foster parents may be considered. (There is a desperate need for both, especially among children who come from difficult circumstances and who have special needs.) Volunteering at schools, food banks, nursing homes, soup kitchens, etc. could also teach spouses without children that their lives as a couple must include service to others. When this happens the marriage is enriched immensely!

Blended Families Couples who are in second and sometimes third marriages, and are trying to bring together children from their previous marriages into their new one, have a daunting challenge. It is not impossible, but it does demand skills in family diplomacy and communication that many families simply do not have.

Dr. Richard Nicastro, explains why blended families have such a difficult time: [20]

Kids will make your second marriage a complicated and challenging experience. The reason is clear: In most circumstances, children do not want their parents to <u>divorce</u>. Therefore, the idea of your meeting someone new and finding <u>happiness</u> is not a priority in the appropriately egocentric world of your child. So your children's view of your new <u>marriage</u> will necessarily be very different from your own.

Children are angry about the loss of their old <u>family</u> and anxious about the creation of a new one. Some children are quite good at hiding these feelings, while others will make their anger known every step of the way. Even if your children genuinely like *your new spouse, you should remember that your son or daughter already has two parents. For many kids, the more they like their new step-parent, the more traitorous they feel toward the biological parent they perceive as being "left behind." Struggles with divided loyalties can lead children to disrupt arrangements between you and your new mate.*

Very often couples blending two families need professional help to do this successfully (see www.step-families.info). Again, this is not impossible. Blended families may not turn out like the Brady Bunch, but two families who are working hard at listening to one another and communicating effectively can live together in peace.

Gift and Work Children do not ask to be born. They were not given the option of choosing their parents or siblings. One of the great challenges that couples face is giving their children a healthy and successful family. I write "healthy and successful," and not "perfect" because perfect families do not exist, but healthy and successful ones do.

Some of the greatest tension we felt during the years of raising our children was between what we insisted they participate in as members of our family – daily supper, chores, prayer time, fun time, trips and extended family events – and the demands placed on them by outside commitments and friends.

Not everyone comes from a happy childhood, but everyone can break from the unhealthy patterns of their childhood to create a new family where love, forgiveness, friendship, teamwork, and joy abound. We do not have a perfect family, but we do have a successful one. A couple of years ago, one of my daughters sent me a Father's Day card, and in it she wrote:

"Besides marrying Mom, what I am most grateful for are the siblings you (and she) gave me."

Children are a great gift, but they are work. And the greatest gift you will ever give to your children is not music, voice, or dance lessons, a college degree, or even an inheritance into a life of comfort and ease; it is your "healthy and successful" marriage.

Our story by Robert: *After we had settled into an NFP routine and the youngest of our three children had turned three years old, we began to sense in prayer that they needed something to bring a spark to their lives. We discussed what that might be – Nintendo, dance lessons, a pet, joining the Y, etc. – But the prompting of the Spirit was really towards another baby*

Baby number four mesmerized her Fontana siblings in ways that nothing else could. She brought wonder into their lives with every new expression on her face, every new trick in crawling, pulling up, and walking, and every new sound that slowly turned into words. The older children wanted to help feed, clothe, hold, and even bathe their sister (but they did not want anything to do with her when her diaper was full).

Shortly after her birth, my brother, who was going through a difficult time, came to live with us. Her impact on him was most profound. He did not have children and had never really been around children, especially babies. I was working nights and weekends, so he would help Lori get the children settled at night by watching the baby as Lori read to the older children.

The only way to describe what happened to my brother is he fell in love. That child opened up his eyes and heart to all that was good in the world. He delighted in everything about her. Watching her was even better than watching college football on TV. By her mere presence as a baby growing into a toddler, our fourth child helped her uncle rediscover joy in his life and was truly essential in helping him transition from a place of hurt and pain to a better life.

Couple Exercise *Complete the "Children Inventory" below that most applies to you; share your answers using My Turn/Your Turn as needed.*

Children Inventory (includes blended family) On a scale from 1-10 indicate your level of agreement with the following statements with a 10 = Yes, 5 = Sometimes, and a 1 = No.

	No				Sometimes					Yes
1) I had a happy childhood.	1	2	3	4	5	6	7	8	9	10
2) My spouse had a happy childhood.	1	2	3	4	5	6	7	8	9	10
3) We agree on a method of family planning.	1	2	3	4	5	6	7	8	9	10
4) We agree on how to raise our children.	1	2	3	4	5	6	7	8	9	10
5) We argue about our children.	1	2	3	4	5	6	7	8	9	10
6) I think my spouse spends enough time with our children.	1	2	3	4	5	6	7	8	9	10
7) We agree on methods of discipline.	1	2	3	4	5	6	7	8	9	10
8) [If your children are teens or young adults] We agree on how to help them to mature.	1	2	3	4	5	6	7	8	9	10
9) I argue with our children.	1	2	3	4	5	6	7	8	9	10
10) We agree on the role of mother.	1	2	3	4	5	6	7	8	9	10
11) We agree on the role of the father.	1	2	3	4	5	6	7	8	9	10
12) I enjoy being with our children.	1	2	3	4	5	6	7	8	9	10
13) Raising children helps me grow as a person.	1	2	3	4	5	6	7	8	9	10
14) I am satisfied with the relationship I have with our children now.	1	2	3	4	5	6	7	8	9	10
15) I know our children's gifts.	1	2	3	4	5	6	7	8	9	10

Blended Families

	No				Sometimes					Yes
16) My stepchildren love and respect me.	1	2	3	4	5	6	7	8	9	10
17) Our two families are blending peacefully.	1	2	3	4	5	6	7	8	9	10

Complete the following sentences: *When I look back and consider our life with our children, I feel* _____ *because...*

When I consider our relationship with our children now, I feel _____ *because...*

Children Inventory (couples <u>without</u> children) On a scale from 1-10 indicate your level of agreement with the following statements with a 10 = Yes, 5 = Sometimes, and a 1 = No.

	No				Sometimes					Yes
1) I had a happy childhood.	1	2	3	4	5	6	7	8	9	10
2) I was loved and accepted as a child.	1	2	3	4	5	6	7	8	9	10
3) My spouse had a happy childhood.	1	2	3	4	5	6	7	8	9	10
4) My spouse was loved and accepted as a child.	1	2	3	4	5	6	7	8	9	10
5) I enjoy being with children.	1	2	3	4	5	6	7	8	9	10
6) I love my nieces and nephews.	1	2	3	4	5	6	7	8	9	10
7) I enjoy my friends' children and often offer to baby-sit.	1	2	3	4	5	6	7	8	9	10
8) I have come to terms with the reasons we do not have children.	1	2	3	4	5	6	7	8	9	10
9) My spouse has come to terms with the reasons we do not have children.	1	2	3	4	5	6	7	8	9	10
10) Our parents and friends have come to terms with our not having children.	1	2	3	4	5	6	7	8	9	10
11) We enjoy helping other people and do so as a couple.	1	2	3	4	5	6	7	8	9	10
12) We are looking forward to growing old together as a couple.	1	2	3	4	5	6	7	8	9	10
13) I have lots of different interests that help me to fully enjoy life.	1	2	3	4	5	6	7	8	9	10
14) I am happy and at peace with where I am in life.	1	2	3	4	5	6	7	8	9	10

Complete the following sentences: *When I look back and consider our life without children, I feel*

_____ *because...*

When I consider our relationship now and think about how we have been a "gift" to others, I feel _____ *because...*

Children Inventory (newly married) On a scale from 1-10 indicate your level of agreement with the following statements with a 10 = Yes, 5 = Sometimes, and a 1 = No

	No				Sometimes				Yes	
1. I was loved and accepted as a child.	1	2	3	4	5	6	7	8	9	10
2. I have good memories from childhood.	1	2	3	4	5	6	7	8	9	10
3. I liked how my parents raised me and want to do with our children what they did with me.	1	2	3	4	5	6	7	8	9	10
4. My spouse was loved as a child.	1	2	3	4	5	6	7	8	9	10
5. My spouse has good memories of his/her childhood.	1	2	3	4	5	6	7	8	9	10
6. I enjoy being with children.	1	2	3	4	5	6	7	8	9	10
7. My spouse wants to have children.	1	2	3	4	5	6	7	8	9	10
8. My spouse looks forward to becoming a parent.	1	2	3	4	5	6	7	8	9	10
9. We've discussed any fears or concerns about having children.	1	2	3	4	5	6	7	8	9	10
10. We agree on the number of children we would like to have.	1	2	3	4	5	6	7	8	9	10
11. Both our families will be a great help in raising children.	1	2	3	4	5	6	7	8	9	10
12. We've carefully considered the merits of using Natural Family Planning.	1	2	3	4	5	6	7	8	9	10
13. We agree on how we will balance work with child-rearing.	1	2	3	4	5	6	7	8	9	10
14. My spouse liked how she/he was raised, and wants to parent like her/his parents.	1	2	3	4	5	6	7	8	9	10
15. We have good friends who will support us as parents.	1	2	3	4	5	6	7	8	9	10

Complete the following sentences: *When I consider the possibility of having children with my spouse some day, I feel* _____ *because…*

One thing we can do now to prepare ourselves to be successful parents is …

CHAPTER 6

Here Comes Everybody - Faith and Community

It was James Joyce who first used the phrase, "Here comes everybody." As I, Lori, recall, he was referring to the Catholic Church and its practice of infant baptism which brought people from all walks of life into the identity of being Catholic, some with very little faith and others with intense faith, and everyone in between.

Christian marriage is something like that because it is <u>not</u> a private affair or ceremony, even though it's treated as such with invitations, rehearsal dinners, wedding gifts and receptions. In truth, marriage is a public event and everyone is invited to honor its significance by supporting the couple in their life-long covenant of self-giving love.

When Rob and I married, we made public vows of fidelity, love, and honor. In doing so, we invited the public, represented through the best man and maid of honor, to help us keep these vows! We did not get to this wedding day all on our own, and we would not succeed after this wedding day all on our own.

<u>Everybody</u> is asked to support us in our marriage because of the public nature of our vows. This includes the U.S. government (especially the IRS), state government, and local school districts, business owners, etc., as well as the single woman who lives next door. Our public vows of marriage direct her to keep her hands off Rob (and, of course, his hands off her) in support of our marriage.

But our wedding was not just a "public" ceremony, it was a sacramental one.

Our Story *Rob and I met through the Catholic campus ministry at LSU. We each had already had deeply personal experiences of God in our lives and were each committed disciples of Jesus as Catholic Christians. We were looking for potential spouses who had a similar faith, and we were ecstatic when we found each other. Our dating drew us closer to Jesus because we dated one another within the relationships, values, symbols, and practices of a vibrant Catholic community. What did this community do for us?*

1. *Inspired us to save sex for marriage (and we did)*

2. *Offered us opportunities to grow in faith and to mature as persons*

3. *Taught us about Jesus and organized small communities to help support us in following him*

4. *Invited us to the Sacraments to worship God, listen to the Word proclaimed, receive the Eucharist, and seek forgiveness for our sins*

5. *Challenged us to share our wealth — be that money, personal gifts and talents, or time — with the poor, sick, elderly, and spiritually abandoned*

6. *Gave us friends who shared our values, especially the Catholic vision for marriage*

7. *Provided us with many examples of successful couples who mentored us in our relationship*

8. *Showed us how to allow the Holy Spirit to direct our lives as a married couple*

9. *Gave us the witness of the saints for inspiration, wisdom, and encouragement*

10. *Provided us with foundational doctrines on which we could build our faith*

11. *And gave us a sacramental worldview that taught us to see the hand of God at work through the relationships and commitments of life*

We brought some very high ideals to our marriage. We wanted our relationship to proclaim the good news that God is real, that God loves every human person, and that God has a plan of salvation for the world. We knew that it was impossible for us to live this out without the direct help of Jesus and the Holy Spirit, and brothers and sisters from the church.

Once, while we were praying before Steven was born, I had a strong sense that God was speaking directly to our worries and fears. "You worry about your job and the birth of your baby.

Know this: you will not be happy in whatever you do unless I have led you there."

Those words have stuck with us and challenged us to continue to seek the will of God for our life together. Sometimes God's will has been very clear to us. One time, after we had saved some money with the hope of using it for Rob to go to graduate school, we received a letter from a priest friend who was working with the poor in Juarez, Mexico. He described the challenge

of providing fresh water for the members of his community. We felt a conviction to help and sent him half of our savings. Graduate school did not happen for another three years, but when it did; Rob received a scholarship for tuition.

One of our favorite memories as a young couple is of praying together in church in Baton Rouge, Louisiana. We certainly did not plan for it to be a special moment. We simply decided to have a "holy hour" with the Lord before going out on a date. We both felt God's love wrap around us like a warm blanket on a cold night.

God showed up, not with any specific message or miracle, just a loving, awesome presence of grace and goodness. I cannot explain it any better than that, but we both felt very close to Jesus and to one another. I suppose that was the lesson: draw close to Jesus together; Jesus will draw us close to one another.

We do not always clearly see God's will for us or sense God's presence in the day-to-day events of our lives. But we are confident that the Holy Spirit is guiding us and giving us the courage and wisdom we need to succeed in our marriage. This is not something we can do on our own. We need Christian community and friendship to be the individuals, couple, and family we want to be in Christ.

During our college years we joined a household community of Catholic students who wanted to be family together. After college we participated in Charismatic prayer communities, parish small groups, and parish ministry teams. In 1994, we formally entered a lay missionary community called the Missionary Cenacle Apostolate (MCA) and have participated in a Cenacle prayer community ever since.

I have often thought that the best gifts we ever gave to our children have been our friends and the members of our church and faith community. These are the women and men that helped us raise our children and modeled for them what it means to be faith-filled people in the world, including how to be successful in marriage.

Research shows that 43% of church marriages end in divorce.[21] But that statistic is a little skewed, because there are many marriages that happen in a church but the couples do not participate in the Church. When the studies zero in on couples who actually attend church, the divorce rate is lower than the national average. The divorce rate for active Catholics, for example, is 23%, and for Christians active in Protestant and Evangelical churches the divorce rate is 32%. Faith communities help couples stay married.[22]

Couples Activity: *Where do you find common ground with your spouse in regards to faith? Who are the people who stand with you as a community of faith? Find out by completing the Faith and Community Inventory separately; then compare one another's answers.*

Use *My Turn/Your Turn* as needed.

Faith and Community Inventory On a scale from 1-10 indicate your level of agreement with the following statements with a 10 = Yes, 5 = Sometimes, and a 1 = No.

	No				Sometimes					Yes
1) I have a personal relationship with Jesus.	1	2	3	4	5	6	7	8	9	10
2) Divorce is an option for me under certain circumstances.	1	2	3	4	5	6	7	8	9	10
3) My spouse and I agree on major articles of faith.	1	2	3	4	5	6	7	8	9	10
4) We have many friends whose marriages we admire and learn from.	1	2	3	4	5	6	7	8	9	10
5) We are giving our children a religious education.	1	2	3	4	5	6	7	8	9	10
6) I enjoy reading the Bible.	1	2	3	4	5	6	7	8	9	10
7) My spouse and I pray together.	1	2	3	4	5	6	7	8	9	10
8) My spouse and I serve the poor together.	1	2	3	4	5	6	7	8	9	10
9) We enjoy attending church together.	1	2	3	4	5	6	7	8	9	10
10) We pray with our children at home.	1	2	3	4	5	6	7	8	9	10
11) We agree on core values.	1	2	3	4	5	6	7	8	9	10
12) I take time for personal prayer.	1	2	3	4	5	6	7	8	9	10
13) We seek God's will for our lives.	1	2	3	4	5	6	7	8	9	10
14) My spouse sacrifices for our marriage.	1	2	3	4	5	6	7	8	9	10
15) My spouse is a spiritual leader in our home.	1	2	3	4	5	6	7	8	9	10

Name three core values you share with your spouse.
1.
2.
3.

Complete the sentence: When I consider the faith and community that we share in our marriage I feel _____ because...

Something that I would like to see happen in regards to faith and community is...

CHAPTER 7

Fidelity, Love, and Honor

In 1963, General Douglas MacArthur spoke to the graduating class at West Point. MacArthur commanded U.S. Army and Navy forces in the South Pacific, leading them to victory over Japan. He oversaw the occupation of Japan following the war and led U.S. troops in the early stages of what would be known as the Korean War. Little did he know that the junior officers he was addressing would soon be leading troops into battle in South Vietnam. The General left a lasting impression on these newly commissioned officers as he reminded them over and over again of the West Point motto:

DUTY, HONOR, COUNTRY!

"Duty, Honor, Country: Those three hallowed words reverently dictate what you ought to be, what you can be, what you will be. They are your rallying points: to build courage when courage seems to fail; to regain faith when there seems to be little cause for faith; to create hope when hope becomes forlorn."[23]

Married couples have a similar motto that guides their actions in good times and bad, in sickness and health:

FIDELITY, LOVE, HONOR!

These are, of course, the vows that spouses make to one another on their wedding day. They summarize precisely how a couple will be able to sustain their commitment to one another over a lifetime.

FIDELITY, LOVE, HONOR!

One version of the marriage vows goes like this:

I, (_____), take you (_____) to be my husband/wife. I promise to be true to you in good times and bad, in sickness and in health. I will love you and honor you all the days of my life.

Most couples, unless they have renewed their vows at an anniversary, or have heard them exchanged at another wedding or in a movie, have given little formal attention to their wedding vows. They sort of sink into the subconscious as the honeymoon ends and work, children, and extracurricular activities take over. Although they move off of a couple's radar screen, marriage vows usually get absorbed into life and have an unspoken existence. These sacred promises remain the foundation upon which successful marriages are built. They especially rise to the surface of a couple's mind during times of trial and struggle.

"They build courage when courage seems to fail; restore faith when there seems to be little cause for faith; and create hope when hope becomes forlorn."

FIDELITY, LOVE, AND HONOR!

Couple Exercise: What do these words mean to you? Think about a definition for each of these words; share your definitions with your spouse.

Vows for Life Some people get married on beaches, others in great cathedrals, and still others in the living room of their parents' home. There was a wedding in Baton Rouge, Louisiana, held at a home that dated back to the Civil War. The wedding carried the theme of the antebellum South and cost over $50,000 (1977 dollars). The women wore Southern hoop skirts and the men were dressed in Confederate officer uniforms.

Our wedding cost $90 of borrowed money for Rob's suit, materials for the dresses of the wedding party made by a dear friend, and the potluck of desserts that friends brought for the reception.

The most important moment of the day is not the dress-up time before the wedding or the party afterwards. It is when bride and groom make public vows before God, family and friends, to be true to one another in good times and bad, and to love and honor one another until separated by death.

Here is a Scripture reading from the book of Tobit that contains the wedding vows in the form of a prayer (Tobit 8:4b-9):

Tobiah arose from bed and said to his wife, "My love, get up. Let us pray and beg our Lord to have mercy on us and to grant us deliverance."

She got up, and they started to pray and beg that deliverance might be theirs. He began with these words: "Blessed are you, O God of our fathers; praised be your name forever and ever. Let the heavens and all your creation praise you forever.

You made Adam and you gave him his wife Eve to be his help and support; and from these two the human race descended. You said, 'It is not good for the man to be alone; let us make him a partner like himself.'

Now, Lord, you know that I take this wife of mine not because of lust, but for a noble purpose. Call down your mercy on me and on her, and allow us to live together to a happy old age."

They said together, "Amen, amen," and went to bed for the night.

At the lowest moment in our marriage, it was our wedding vows that we stood on when something had to change. And during those moments of amazing joy when everything is going right and we fit together like a pair of well-worn slippers, it is those wedding vows that we celebrate. In fact, we often verbally renew our wedding vows after we have had a romantic encounter in the bedroom!

Gary Smalley, in his video series, *Hidden Keys to Loving Relationships,* states that the most important of the three vows, and the path to the other two, is "honor." Catholics instinctively know what honor means. It is how we treat the Blessed Sacrament by genuflecting in church, saving conversations for

outside of church, bowing when we walk past the tabernacle, and spending moments in silent prayer before it.

That is the sort of esteem and respect we are called to give one another in marriage. When a husband is treated with such honor by his wife, it opens his heart to fidelity and love. And when a wife is treated with such honor by her husband, it opens her heart to fidelity and love.

"I will be true to you" is a vow of faithfulness, but this implies more than spouses not being physically or even emotionally invested in another man or woman. In our busy world where traditional roles and expectations have little meaning, fidelity in marriage means keeping current with one's spouse, with one's thoughts, feelings, desires, etc., especially those pertaining to the relationship. Couples that do not communicate regularly on how they are getting along will not survive in the fast-paced world of the 21st century. Regular communication, which really means daily, is imperative.

We check in with one another every night on how each other's day has been, what has been good and not-so-good, and even on how we are doing as a couple.

The vow of love is not a vow to always feel intense emotions of affection and desire for one another over a life-time. In fact, the vow of love has little to do with feelings. This is an "action vow," to do whatever is 100% in the best interest of your spouse and of the marriage. The priest at our wedding put it this way:

If there is anything in your power that you can do that you know will make the other happy, do it.

Certainly each vow needs the others, compliments the others, and enlarges the others. Together they make marriage possible.

Couple Exercise: Complete the Vow Assessment separately and share your answers. Use *My Turn/ Your Turn* as needed.

Vow Inventory On a scale from 1-10 indicate your level of agreement with the following statements with a 10 = Yes, 5 = Sometimes, and a 1 = No.

	No				Sometimes					Yes
1. My spouse tells me about what he/she is doing.	1	2	3	4	5	6	7	8	9	10
2. My spouse does not allow any person, place, or thing to be more important than our marriage.	1	2	3	4	5	6	7	8	9	10
3. I do not allow any person, place, or thing to be more important than our relationship.	1	2	3	4	5	6	7	8	9	10
4. My spouse tells me what he/she is thinking.	1	2	3	4	5	6	7	8	9	10
5. My spouse keeps our intimate life private.	1	2	3	4	5	6	7	8	9	10
6. My spouse gives me the space I need to take care of myself.	1	2	3	4	5	6	7	8	9	10
7. My spouse accepts me for who I am and doesn't try to change me.	1	2	3	4	5	6	7	8	9	10
8. I'm a good listener and do not try to always have the last word.	1	2	3	4	5	6	7	8	9	10
9. My spouse shows me great respect and honor.	1	2	3	4	5	6	7	8	9	10
10. My spouse anticipates my needs and helps me.	1	2	3	4	5	6	7	8	9	10
11. My spouse is kind and good to my family.	1	2	3	4	5	6	7	8	9	10
12. My spouse has appropriate boundaries with the opposite sex.	1	2	3	4	5	6	7	8	9	10
13. I struggle with pornography.	1	2	3	4	5	6	7	8	9	10
14. I'm offended when my spouse looks at porn.	1	2	3	4	5	6	7	8	9	10
15. I'm unafraid to raise difficult topics with my spouse.	1	2	3	4	5	6	7	8	9	10
16. My spouse is always ready to resolve differences and apologizes when necessary.	1	2	3	4	5	6	7	8	9	10

When I consider how we try to be faithful to our vows I feel _____ because…

CHAPTER 8

The Imperfect Couple

There are no perfect couples. There are only imperfect couples who are committed to sharing a lifetime together in good times and in bad, in sickness and in health; imperfect couples who keep the vows of fidelity, love and honor imperfectly.

Many times, without even meaning to, we hurt one another simply because we didn't say something quite the way we wanted to, expectations were not met, or, worse, we were ticked off and did exactly what we knew would get our spouse's dander up.

> ***Our Story*** *We have not always seen eye-to-eye on how to deal with the children in certain situations. Lori was usually the bad cop, Rob the…quiet cop.*
>
> *We have different visions of what a restful weekend looks like. Rob would like to bike 20 miles and work in the garden; Lori would like to pay the bills and read a book.*
>
> *Lori hates surprises and surprise parties, and Rob loves them. Lori loves Valentine's Day, and Rob took years to pick up on that. Rob loves the national holidays and flying the flag; Lori has come around to that.*
>
> *Lori remembers everything that she is asked to do and does so promptly. Rob remembers some of the things that he is asked to do and gets done most of what he remembers.*
>
> *Rob keeps fun, romance, and prayer alive in the family; Lori keeps everyone safe and Rob "out of jail," insuring taxes, insurance, and parking fines are paid. Our different "gifts" often compliment one another, but sometimes they clash. Forgiveness has been another "glue" that has held our marriage together.*

Here is Jesus' parable about forgiveness (Matthew 18: 21-35) adapted for the imperfect couple:

Then Peter approaching asked him, "Lord, if my [spouse] sins against me, how often must I forgive her? As many as seven times?" Jesus answered, "I say to you, not seven times but seventy-seven times.

That is why the kingdom of heaven may be likened to a husband who accidentally woke his wife while leaving early one morning for work. He apologized and left with his lunch that she made.

She got up and realized that she had forgotten to prepare coffee for him to take. She called him and apologized, but asked if he would pick up some bread for dinner. He agreed to, but apologized for not telling her last night that her mother had called and would like for her to call back as soon as possible.

When he returned home at night he had the bread, but also he brought home a guest for supper. "Please forgive me" he said to his wife, "I thought I had told you over the phone today."

While they were eating, her mother called and she answered, spending the entire dinner time talking on the phone. She apologized for not telling her mom that they were eating and that she would call her back.

At the end of the day, after the guest had left, the husband and wife climbed into bed to say their prayers. They turned to each other and said, "Please forgive me for not loving you as I should." And each responded, "I forgive you."

My heavenly Father will forgive you as you forgive each other from the heart.

Couple Exercise: *Review the above paragraphs; what stands out for you?*

What's your pet peeve at home?

What's your spouse's pet peeve at home?

Forgiveness Many people have a misunderstanding about what forgiveness is and what it is not. Forgiveness <u>is not</u> the same as reconciliation. Reconciliation happens in any relationship, especially marriage, when there has been some measure of <u>restored trust</u>. Restored trust takes time, especially when there has been a serious breach of that trust, and it usually happens in stages.

Forgiveness is quite different. For one, forgiveness is something I do for me. The lack of forgiveness is certainly a barrier to restoring trust, but it is something that harms me more than the person I may be angry with.

When I have been hurt in a relationship, and I stew over the hurt until it becomes bitterness and resentment, the bitterness and resentment becomes a cancer that eats a hole in my soul. I may never be able to reconcile with the person who hurt me, but for my sake, I must forgive that person, let go of the desire for retaliation and for getting back at him or her, and wish that person well. An example of this might be a person who betrayed your trust, but died or moved far away. Reconciliation is not possible, but forgiveness is.

Forgiveness does not mean forgetting. That is a recipe for abuse. Leah was beaten up by her husband. She was finally able to leave him with the help of friends. And she was able to forgive him with the help of spiritual mentors, but as long as he continued his drinking and violent behavior, she kept herself and their children far away from him.

Forgiveness means letting go of the hurt in the memory, but not the memory. A friend recently told us that she was badly abused as a child. It was not until she was able to forgive her abuser as an adult that she quit acting like a "victim," powerless against powerful people. Forgiveness gave her the freedom to move on from being an abuse victim to an abuse survivor.

Forgiveness also does not mean "no consequences." We need to hold people accountable for the hurt they cause us. If your teenage son wrecks the car, as ours did, you will forgive him, but he will pay for the damages, as ours did, and you will track his use of the car very closely until you are confident that he can be trusted, as we did.

Couple Exercise *Review the reflection on forgiveness. What do you agree with? What do you disagree with? Talk to each other.*

A Story of Forgiveness Some people wonder if it is possible to forgive another person in the middle of fighting and turmoil. They think that forgiveness can only happen after the conflict is over. However, with the help of God, forgiveness is possible at any moment of the "war." This story is taken from *The First Hero: The Extraordinary Story of Doolittle's Raid*, by Craig Nelson. Nelson tells the story of the first bombing raid against Japan in 1942 by American pilots. Some of these "Dolittle Raiders" were shot down and captured, but most escaped through China.

One American raider who survived the war was Jacob DeShazer. He was captured, tortured, starved, and kept in virtual solitary confinement for three years before he was allowed to have a Bible. He devoured the pages. He knew he would die soon, and prayed, "Lord, though I am far from home and though I am in prison, I must have forgiveness." God's presence filled the room, and Jake was overcome with a tremendous sensation.

"My heart was filled with joy…God had forgiven my sins…hunger, starvation, and a freezing cold prison cell no longer had horrors for me."

The more he read Scripture and reflected on the forgiveness that he had received, Jake knew that he too had to forgive his captors in spite of their brutal abuse. He forgave his jailor and practiced loving and befriending him and, with the little Japanese that he had picked up, became the man's friend. Jake later wrote, *"God had given me new spiritual eyes, and when I looked at the Japanese officers and guards who had starved and beaten me and my companions so cruelly, I found my bitter hatred for them changed to loving pity."*[24]

Another Story of Forgiveness (This story comes from friends whose names I have changed.) Jane and John Doe had been married for a number of years before God blessed them with children. Jane's time and energy were thrown into the children; John worked hard at his job, but always made time for the family on weekends.

Jane and John went to Sunday Mass and even attended Bible study with friends. But tension began to grow between them. They had little time for one another, plus John seemed to be anxious about the business. He was falling behind and needed to go into work early to catch up. Jane had a busy work load too and would often stay late at work until after John had gone to bed. Though John was actually working early in the morning, Jane was not; she was having an affair with a co-worker.

This went on for over a year until guilt got the better of her, and she was truly fearful of losing her family including her husband. She finally broke off the relationship and told John.

John was devastated. His trust in Jane had been absolute. Jane assured him that the other relationship was over, that she did not want to lose him or the children, but the damage was done, and it was immense. John poured venom onto Jane; Jane took it, feeling great shame and remorse.

However, each of them, in their own ways, turned to God and Christian friends for support. They both knew that they wanted to save the marriage; they both knew that God could bring good from evil; they both had intense feelings of hate and shame to work through.

John – *God was my constant companion through all this. I hung on to his word in Scripture and when my feelings overwhelmed me I read out loud those words to defeat the hate and bitterness for Jane that seemed to be taking over. I forgave Jane daily and asked God for the help to forgive her when I felt like I could not.*

Jane – *I hated myself. I had betrayed everything that I had believed in, and hurt the one person in the world that truly loved me for who I am, and I loved him. I cried buckets of tears of shame and remorse. Before I could even accept John's forgiveness I thought I had to forgive myself, but I could not. I just wanted to punish me for being such a jerk. It was John's forgiveness for me that allowed me to forgive myself.*

Jane and John went to a very skilled Christian counselor who helped them rebuild their marriage. Forgiveness, John's forgiving Jane, Jane's forgiving herself, was their path to marriage restoration.

Jane and John not only had to forgive one another, they both went to confession to seek Sacramental forgiveness from their community of faith. Their troubled marriage did not only hurt each other, it also undermined the witness of the Catholic community to marriage so it was most appropriate that they confess their failings and sins in the Sacrament of Reconciliation.

Couple Exercise

Review the stories of forgiveness. What stands out for you? What do these stories say to your marriage?

Complete the Imperfect Couple and Forgiveness Inventory separately. Share your answers with one another. Use My Turn/Your Turn as needed.

The Imperfect Couple/Forgiveness Inventory On a scale from 1-10 indicate your level of agreement with the following statements with a 10 = Yes, 5 = Sometimes, and a 1 = No.

	No				Sometimes					Yes
1. My spouse overworks at his/her job.	1	2	3	4	5	6	7	8	9	10
2. I overwork at my job.	1	2	3	4	5	6	7	8	9	10
3. My spouse is happy with his/her work.	1	2	3	4	5	6	7	8	9	10
4. We are both satisfied with the distribution of chores at home.	1	2	3	4	5	6	7	8	9	10
5. We argue over money and how it is spent.	1	2	3	4	5	6	7	8	9	10
6. I am satisfied with the education and training I have received to do my work.	1	2	3	4	5	6	7	8	9	10
7. Clutter at home is a problem for our marriage.	1	2	3	4	5	6	7	8	9	10
8. We make major decisions about our marriage life jointly.	1	2	3	4	5	6	7	8	9	10
9. My spouse is quick to forgive.	1	2	3	4	5	6	7	8	9	10
10. Alcohol abuse is a problem in our marriage.	1	2	3	4	5	6	7	8	9	10
11. Drug abuse is a problem in our marriage.	1	2	3	4	5	6	7	8	9	10
12. Gambling is a problem in our marriage.	1	2	3	4	5	6	7	8	9	10
13. Over-eating is a problem in our marriage.	1	2	3	4	5	6	7	8	9	10
14. My spouse has told me that I am too controlling.	1	2	3	4	5	6	7	8	9	10
15. I trust my spouse to be honest with me.	1	2	3	4	5	6	7	8	9	10
16. My spouse is able to control his/her temper.	1	2	3	4	5	6	7	8	9	10
17. My spouse is critical of me.	1	2	3	4	5	6	7	8	9	10
18. My spouse has been violent with me, either with words or physically hurting me.	1	2	3	4	5	6	7	8	9	10

19. My spouse is able to admit his/her mistakes.   1   2   3   4   5   6   7   8   9   10

20. My spouse is strongly influenced by others.   1   2   3   4   5   6   7   8   9   10

For Reflection:

Identify the ways that you are most likely to hurt your spouse.

_____Negative words   _____Not listening   _____Taking her/him for granted

_____Withdrawing   _____Avoiding   _____Yelling_____Forgetfulness

_____Undermining agreements   _____Inattentive_____Disregarding feelings

_____Being critical   _____Complaining _Working too much _____Flirting

_____Throwing things or hitting   _____Substance abuse   _____Withdrawing affection

_____Other _____

Identify the ways that your spouse is most likely to hurt you.

_____Negative words_____Not listening   _____Taking her/him for granted

_____Withdrawing _Avoiding_____Yelling_____Forgetfulness

_____Undermining agreements   _____Inattentive_____Disregarding feelings

_____Being critical   _____Complaining   _____Working too much___Flirting

_____Throwing things or hitting   _____Substance abuse   _____Lack of affection

_____Other _____

Complete the sentence:

When I think about how we have hurt one another in our marriage and how we work on forgiving one another, I feel_____ because...

A good memory I have of one or both of us asking for forgiveness and being reconciled is...

Something(s) for which I would like to ask for forgiveness is (are)...

CHAPTER 9

Marriage Is Good for Sex

Among Christians, there is a long history of suspicion about the goodness of sexual pleasure in marriage. Protestant Puritanism and Catholic Jansenism each held that sex in marriage was solely for the purpose of having babies. It was not uncommon for devout Catholic mothers to warn their daughters before the wedding day of the evils of sexual pleasure, as Robert's grandma told his mother: "*It's a sin for women to enjoy sex in marriage; men can because they are weak.*"

Pope Pius XII, in a talk given on October 29, 1951, said that through sex (he actually said "generative function," but he meant sex) "spouses should experience pleasure and enjoyment of body and spirit. Therefore, the spouses do nothing evil in seeking this pleasure and enjoyment." (CCC, #2362) This statement was long overdue!

Thankfully, attitudes about sexual pleasure in marriage are changing for the better. Pleasure during romantic encounters between spouses is important. Who would eat three meals a day if the food did not taste good? If food was not tasty and pleasurable, we would take it in like medicine, good for you and necessary, but hard to swallow. The same is obviously true for sex in marriage. It is important that it be pleasurable. Perhaps that is why women have a clitoris which apparently has <u>no other function</u> than to stimulate sexual pleasure.

Sadly, if you listened to the jokes about marriage you would conclude that tying the knot kills great sex.

"*Three Irish men, Pat, Mike, and Sean, are playing golf on an unseasonably warm day in December. Says Pat to the others, "Lads, if the weather is like this on Christmas Day, I'd take it as a sign from the child Jesus that he wants us to meet for a round of golf.*"

They all agreed, but Sean cautioned them, "It may be that the child Jesus wants us to play, but our wives may not. And each of us may have to pay a high price to persuade them."

The other two agreed. On Christmas morning the weather was mild and sunny, and the men met at the clubhouse eager to celebrate the birth of the Christ child with a round of golf. Says Pat to Mike, "And what did it cost you to come today?"

"A new kitchen table with chairs but here I am."

"And you, Sean," says Pat, "What did it cost you to come today?"

"A great big diamond on a ring but here I am."

"And you?" say Sean and Mike to Pat, "What did it cost you to come today?"

"Not a penny!"

"No?"

"Yes!"

"I told me wife, 'Love, it is Christmas morn. Either we make love or I play a round of golf with the lads.' And here I am."

The jokes are funny, but they are wrong; <u>marriage</u> is good for <u>sex</u>. Marriage gives sexual energy the boundaries it needs to enable it to enrich intimacy and seal the bond of love between couples. Maggie Waite and Linda Gallagher, in their book *The Case for Marriage*, cite studies that compare the sexual behavior of married couples, cohabiting couples, singles who have never been married, and singles who are divorced. In the four major categories examined - frequency of sex, enjoyment of sex, creativity in sex, and meaning of sex - married couples excelled.[25]

Here's a summary of their findings.

Frequency of Sex — Cohabiting couples report having the most sexual encounters per week (2-3 times); married couples run a close second (twice a week). Contrary to the public image, "swinging singles" have to work hard at getting a sexual partner. They have to spend time primping, meet a potential partner at a night spot, spend money on drinks and dinner, and hope for romance later. Married and cohabiting couples just have to roll over.

Commitment Is Sexy — Frequency of sex is about the only advantage that cohabiting couples have over those who are in it for life. According to Waite and Gallagher, the "cohabiters" are missing out on plenty. For one, commitment, apparently, is very sexy. Studies show that when couples make a commitment to one another, such as an engagement and marriage, the pleasure of sex increases immensely. This is true for women <u>and</u> men, but especially women.

When she knows that he is going to be around for the long haul and he knows the same, they both discover a great freedom to relax and fully give of themselves to one another during their romantic forays. Furthermore, they learn that if during one night of romance the sex just fizzles, fear not; an opportunity will soon come for it to "sizzle."

Creativity and Sexual Intimacy — In fact, because married couples promise to be exclusive in their sexual commitment to one another, spouses learn to trust one another with what each enjoys. Telling a spouse what is pleasurable or not pleasurable can be very difficult. It takes great trust between spouses to be so vulnerable, but when this happens, couples experiment, get creative and, over time, expand their sexual repertoire.

The Meaning of Sexual Intimacy — Most people want sex to mean something, and married sex, whether it is an evening with candlelight, massage, soft kisses, and intimate romance or a quick encounter on the couch, means a reaffirmation of the wedding vows:

I will be true to you in good times and bad, sickness and health, and I will love you and honor you all the days of my life.

For Catholics, marriage is one of the seven sacraments. A sacrament is a physical sign, something one can see, touch, and smell (for example; water or bread) that reveals a hidden, unseen reality. In the case of Baptism, water is the sign of cleansing and forgiveness of sin. In the case of the Eucharist, bread is the sign of Jesus as spiritual food.

The sacramental sign of marriage is sexual intimacy. The physical union of spouses in sexual intercourse shows outwardly what is happening in a hidden way: the joining of these two persons into one body, one flesh. Every time a married couple "makes love," whether it is a wild moment of uncontrolled passion, or a relaxed evening of intimacy, that couple is renewing their wedding vows, for this is the meaning of "sex in marriage."

Challenges: Men and Women Have Different Needs Around Sexual Intimacy — Of course, not all of our experiences around sex and sexual interaction are wonderful and pleasurable. For instance, many men apparently complain that there is not enough sex in their marriage, and many women complain that there is not enough affection in their love-making and wonder why all romantic moments must lead to the big S (SEX).

There's an old saying that boys use love to get sex and that girls use sex to get love. Does that pattern continue in married life? Apparently so, says Dr. Kevin Leman in his book, *Sex Begins in the Kitchen*. He writes that the greatest need for men in their relationship with their wives is "sexual fulfillment." However, the greatest need for women in their relationship with their husbands is "affection."[26]

Do men want affection too? Of course, but they want it through a satisfying and fulfilling sexual relationship with their wives. In fact, according to Shaunti and Jeff Feldhahn, in *For Men Only*, many men take it very personally when their wives say, "Not tonight." Jeff writes, "Men are powerfully driven by the emotional need to feel desired by our wives and we filter everything through that grid… If we feel our wife truly wants us sexually, we feel confident, powerful, alive, and loved. If we don't, we feel depressed, angry, and alone."

Do women want a satisfying and fulfilling sex life? Of course, but what they want most is emotional connection and affection. A woman's desire for sex is not <u>as</u> connected to the "desirability of her husband" as it is to her hormones and monthly menstrual cycle. Most women feel greater physical desires for sex during ovulation, the very time when they will most likely get pregnant if they have sexual intercourse. The days before and after ovulation are generally low hormonal days for women, with not much sexual energy. It may take plenty of foreplay and affection for a busy woman, with children to care for and a list of things to do, to get interested in sex with her spouse during these "dry periods."

According to the Feldhahns, in a survey question that asked women about the one thing they most wanted their husbands to know, 96 percent of the respondents made statements such as, "Just because I do not want sex as often as he does, I still love him deeply and find him very attractive. I just have a lower sex drive than he does," and "I'm sometimes simply too tired or stressed," and "It's sometimes hard to make the transition to wanting physical intimacy."

Advice columnist Ann Landers was challenged by a reader, "If you were to ask 100 women how they feel about sexual intercourse, 98 would say, "Just hold me close and tender. Forget about the act." Ann took up the challenge and asked her women readers: "Send a postcard or letter with a reply to the question: Would you be content to be held close and treated tenderly and forget about "the act?" Reply YES or NO and please add one line. "I am over (or under) 40 years of age."

Her findings? More than 90,000 women cast their ballots. 72 percent said yes, they would be content to be held close and treated tenderly and to forget about the act. Of those 72 percent who said yes, 40 percent were under 40 years old. The greatest need for women in marriage is "affection." [27]

What about married men? Are they satisfied with just affection? NO! They want "sexual fulfillment!" That does not mean they just want the "act." They want a mutually engaging sexual relationship that is fun, regular, pleasurable, and fulfilling. This is especially true for men as they age and mature, and learn to give and receive from their spouses in sexual love.

Other Challenges and Tensions — Many people bring plenty of negative baggage to their sex lives. This is true for Christians who have been raised with strong convictions that anything as pleasurable as sex must be a sin just as Robert's grandma believed.

Body Image — Many women and men bring to their marital lovemaking a very negative body image. This seems to be a greater problem for women, but men have their "body-image" challenges as well. All of us who have grown up with images of Barbie, Marilyn Monroe, Halle Berry, and Angelina Jolie as the prototypes for a beautiful woman and John Wayne, Robert Redford, Denzel Washington, and Brad Pitt as the prototypes for a handsome man have at one time or another struggled with body image.

Healthy teens becoming adults, so as to avoid the pitfall of self-hate regarding their bodies, learn to apply the Serenity Prayer to their body image:

God grant me the serenity to accept the things I cannot change; courage to change the things I can; and wisdom to know the difference.

One of the great gifts that a spouse gives to his or her marriage partner in sexual intimacy is acceptance of his or her body as it is. This is a delicate topic, to say the least. One friend reported to us how hard it was to be intimate with his wife because she was very overweight, and he simply did not find her attractive. They had some difficult conversations around this and other issues in their relationship that led her to find comfort in eating, but weight was something she could change. He changed some of his negative ways of relating to her, and she lost some weight.

Sexual and Physical Abuse - To complicate the body image problem, many men and women who were physically and sexually abused as children and teenagers, have difficulty with sexual intimacy as adults. A male friend who was abused as a child told us how much he struggles with trust and confidence in his sexual relationship with his wife. A woman friend who had been abused found it hard to have her husband touch her in any way that hinted at sexual intimacy.

Same Sex Attraction – Human sexuality is a fluid phenomenon. There is absolutely no scientific evidence that humans are born "gay" or "straight." One's sexuality and sexual attraction develop in childhood through a complex interaction between genetic predispositions, environmental factors, and a multitude of moment-to-moment choices that an individual makes that shape the person he or she is becoming.[28] The vast majority of children develop a heterosexual orientation to their sexuality, a small percentage are drawn to both men and women in their sexual orientation, and a still smaller percentage are firmly set in a same sex orientation.[29]

It is not uncommon for a spouse who is married and very capable of enjoying sexual intimacy to also struggle with same-sex attractions. This does not mean the end of the marriage! Nor does it mean that the spouse dealing with same-sex-attraction simply has to deny these feelings, and suffer through marriage with an unfulfilled sex life.

Negative body images, physical and sexual abuse, and same-sex attractions are not insurmountable issues for spouses to overcome, but they must be discussed, usually with professional help, and be addressed as openly and honestly as possible.[30]

Women Have Special Needs — Many women also report that sexual intercourse does not do "it" for them. Without some manual stimulation of the clitoris, they are unable to reach sexual climax. And for sexual intimacy to be mutually fulfilling for most

couples, it is important that women be able to satisfy their sexual desires in a way similar to men, with an orgasm. Husbands can sometimes think they are doing something wrong when their wives are unable to climax through sexual intercourse.

Some couples have religious scruples about genital stimulation. Technically, for Catholics to comply with Church teaching on sexuality, spouses can touch one another in every possible way, including genital stimulation, as long as their sexual interaction concludes with sexual intercourse.[31]

Men Have Special Needs Too - Sexual dysfunction for men is complicated. Age, excessive alcohol or drug intake, poor diet, or depression may cause it. It may also be caused by health issues like diabetes, obesity, accidents to the spinal column, or a stroke. It is important that husbands speak to their wives about any sexual dysfunction they might be experiencing, and that they seek help from a medical doctor. Sometimes the solution is as simple as getting a good night's sleep and learning to be more affectionate in lovemaking.

Sexual Intimacy and Natural Family Planning
Many Catholics and other Christians have found Natural Family Planning (NFP) to be a great aid in intensifying the enjoyment of sexual intimacy because it teaches couples about one another's bodies and how to speak to each other about their sexual needs. Yes, NFP keeps the ever-present relationship between sex and pregnancy at the forefront of married love. Most importantly, it helps husbands to learn to discipline their sexual energies for the good of the marriage.

Men need to learn to bring self-control to the ever-demanding sexual desires that churn within their bodies. Even for couples that use artificial birth control, husbands cannot always have sex on demand. There are many times when they are not able to have sex with their spouses because of illness, exhaustion, separation, etc. At these times they need to practice sexual discipline. Practicing NFP teaches men to discipline their sexual energy and find other ways than sexual intercourse, to physically connect with their spouses.

We practiced NFP and are grateful for how it helped us to strengthen our relationship and give birth to our six children with reasonable spacing between them. NFP is not easy. It does take motivation, the support of friends, and a spiritual life to practice it with any success. A 1994 survey suggested that only about four percent of Catholics practice Natural Family Planning.[32] Some couples who practice NFP have found that it created certain challenges for a satisfying sexual life. Fear of pregnancy can inhibit sexual desires among some women using NFP, and having a large family can place demands on a couple's energy, leaving little left for romance.

Some NFP users are frustrated with the reality that the very time the woman has strong desires for sexual intimacy, during ovulation; they must refrain from sex unless they are open to the possibility of conception.

These are not insurmountable challenges, but they are real issues that NFP couples face, and they can do so successfully if they talk to one another.

The Challenge of Porn — Pornography can kill a sexual relationship between spouses. Pamela Paul writes in *The Porn Factor,* "At the 2003 meeting of the American Academy of Matrimonial Lawyers, two-thirds of the 350 divorce lawyers who attended said the Internet played a significant role in divorces, with excessive interest in online porn contributing to more than half of such cases."

One couple who sought us out for help in strengthening their marriage kept coming back to "porn" being the major issue they faced. The wife said to us, "As long as he has all his other women, he doesn't need me." A husband from another couple who was attending a marriage workshop told us that he has been so absorbed with porn that he cannot find any sexual arousal with his spouse who was an attractive woman.

Porn causes the viewer to objectify the individuals in the photos, seeing them as a collection of body parts, and allowing the viewer to live in a fantasy world where the demands of a relationship with a real person are non-existent. Women view porn, but not nearly as much as men. For example, some studies show that half of the readership of *Playgirl,* a magazine for women featuring photos of nude men, is gay men.[33]

A Good Night's Sleep — The pre-condition for a healthy sexual life, aside from a healthy relationship, is a good night's sleep, exercise, and a balanced diet. Busy lives and the demands of children leave most couples sleep deprived. Throw in lack of exercise and poor diets, stress and aging issues, and we have couples struggling with sexual intimacy. A healthy sexual life that is mutually satisfying for both wife and husband does not just happen on the wedding night. It takes fidelity, trust, and honor, good communication skills, and a commitment to keeping sexual intimacy a priority for couples to experience a pattern of enjoyment and pleasure with sex in their marriage.

Couple Exercise: *Review the above article. Talk to your spouse about anything that stands out for you. Afterwards complete the Sexual Intimacy Inventory separately and discuss your answers. Use My Turn/Your Turn as needed.*

Sexual Intimacy Inventory On a scale from 1-10 indicate your level of agreement with the following statements with a 10 = Yes, 5 = Sometimes, and a 1 = No.

	No				Sometimes					Yes
1) I am satisfied with our sex life.	1	2	3	4	5	6	7	8	9	10
2) I was raised with a healthy attitude about sex.	1	2	3	4	5	6	7	8	9	10
3) My spouse is comfortable with his/her sexuality.	1	2	3	4	5	6	7	8	9	10
4) I often prefer intimacy that does not lead to sexual intercourse.	1	2	3	4	5	6	7	8	9	10
5) Romance is alive and well in our marriage.	1	2	3	4	5	6	7	8	9	10
6) I can tell my spouse what I like and dislike in love-making.	1	2	3	4	5	6	7	8	9	10
7) I enjoy sex with my spouse.	1	2	3	4	5	6	7	8	9	10
8) My spouse knows how I like to be touched.	1	2	3	4	5	6	7	8	9	10
9) I am satisfied with how many times we have sex each week.	1	2	3	4	5	6	7	8	9	10
10) We are affectionate with one another outside the bedroom.	1	2	3	4	5	6	7	8	9	10
11) Fear of getting pregnant does not interfere with our sex life.	1	2	3	4	5	6	7	8	9	10
12) We agree on methods of family planning.	1	2	3	4	5	6	7	8	9	10
13) I did not have any bad experiences related to sex as a child or teenager.	1	2	3	4	5	6	7	8	9	10
14) I do not think sexual pleasure is sinful.	1	2	3	4	5	6	7	8	9	10
15) I know what my spouse enjoys during lovemaking.	1	2	3	4	5	6	7	8	9	10
16) Our sexual relationship is mutually pleasurable.	1	2	3	4	5	6	7	8	9	10

Complete the following sentence: When I consider our sexual life I feel _____
because...

Something we could do to strengthen our sexual intimacy is...

CHAPTER 10

Money Matters

The New Testament does not have a very positive view of money. Jesus said that no one can serve two masters. *"He will either hate one and love the other, or be devoted to one and despise the other."* (Matthew 6:24) He was referring to money. Money has an ugly habit of becoming a person's master. St. Paul says this about money:

"The love of money is the root of all evils, and some people in their desire for it have strayed from the faith and have pierced themselves with many pains."(1 Timothy 6:10)

Money does matter. It is important, but it is not most important. It can be like a poisonous snake that must be handled with care lest we are bitten and the poison of self-centered power is unleashed in our veins!

Our Story, by Lori That, however, was not our problem with money. We under-appreciated the value of money. This was especially true of Robert. He wanted to live simply as St. Francis did, trusting that God would care for us as God does for the "birds of the air" and the "flowers in the field." Rob was slow to catch on about how expensive children are and the proper place of money.

Yes, of course, God did care for us as we began our life together, with Rob working at a large Catholic parish in southern Louisiana and making a... (How can I write this politely?) ...a modest salary. We lived in a shack that was hotter inside than outside during the summer months, and just as cold inside as outside during the winter months. You can imagine that we had visitors only during the fall and spring.

We made ends meet mostly through the generosity of our family and faith community who occasionally dropped off bags of groceries, or slipped us a donation underneath the door, or took us out to dinner. But, since we were still on the learning curve for Natural Family Planning, we knew children were coming. This method of Franciscan financial planning could not continue. We knew how to deny ourselves many material items for the sake of living simply. We had to learn how to insist on just salaries from our Catholic employers, and incorporate the children's needs for swim lessons, musical instruments and music lessons, health insurance, travel to see family, Christmas and birthday gifts, and, yikes, retirement into our commitment to live simply so that we could devote our energies towards family, friendships, and serving the poor.

The watershed moment for us, and Rob in particular, happened when our daughter Mary was born. She had discoloring in one ear, a large hemangioma on her forehead, with long flowing hair on one side of her head, and short typical baby hair on the other. Our pediatrician diagnosed it correctly but with such alarming consequences: "She'll have to have laser surgery to get rid of that hemangioma, and it will be very bloody!" I was scared to death!

We spent the next year visiting one specialist after another — and each interpreted Mary's condition differently. We eventually went to a clinic in New Orleans that brought together a number of specialists who agreed with the original diagnosis but not the treatment plan.

"Don't do anything. Monitor it and by the time she's a teenager, if it doesn't take care of itself, come back."

The upshot of this, money-wise, was that we had to confront the difficult truth: Rob's salary and our insurance plan were woefully inadequate for a growing family. We had to take the topic of money and making money for the support of our family much more seriously, which meant that Rob had to learn to lobby his clergy employers for wages and benefits commensurate with his education, training, and the demands of the job.

We've had some arguments over money, but not so severe as to threaten our marriage. Usually our arguments were over how to stretch what little we had to cover the many competing needs, or how Rob was going to get a part-time job to help compensate his church salary. I was <u>working</u> at home caring for the six children and managing the home.

I do not know how we learned this, but we did learn early on to avoid credit card debt and have never struggled with that wet blanket over our life together. We have shopped at Goodwill, Value Village and St. Vincent de Paul for our clothes, planted a garden for vegetables, eaten little meat and lots of beans, rice, and bread, and simplified Christmas to not only make ends meet, but to have something to share with the poor through our tithe.

When I think back on our relationship with money, even though we did have to mature in learning its proper value, we were united from the beginning around the idea that God was the real "owner" of our money. If we lived simply, we could meet the financial needs of our family, as well as serve the poor through tithing, and teach the children to do the same.

Couple Exercise: *What importance did your parents place on money?*

What value did you place on money when you were dating and newly married?

How has that changed over the years?

What have you taught your children about the value of money? Talk to one another.

SOME THOUGHTS ABOUT MONEY

The struggle over money in a marriage is often a struggle over "power and control" in the relationship. Martin Luther King, Jr. once wrote, "I am not interested in power for power's sake, but I'm interested in power that is moral, that is right and that is good." He and the Civil Rights Movement wanted "power" to do good and be a power for good — especially for African Americans who had for so long been locked out of the power factions in America.

Power can be used for good or ill. Nuclear power can be used to light a city or destroy it. For many people, "money" equals "power." Money is the primary way for people in American culture to gain some measure of independence and ability to do what they want for themselves and for others. Money is <u>power</u> in society in general and, specifically, in marriage. And the fight over money in marriage is cited as the number one reason for divorce.

When a woman and a man marry, they not only join their bodies in sexual love, they join their money in a legally binding relationship that makes each responsible for the other's debt in a court of law. This spousal relationship around money is often more complicated than the sexual one, especially when there are two incomes to manage. (We have a joint account.)

Working out how to spend that money can be a battle fraught with many hidden issues that stem from a spouse's sense of his or her power in the marriage. These "hidden issues" usually relate to deep human needs for security, hope, safety, love, and acceptance.

Having control over all the money, or at least some of the money, gives a spouse some control in meeting those deeper, unspoken needs. Today it is not uncommon for couples to have completely separate bank accounts to minimize any collision of needs and "power struggles" over how those needs are to be met, though legally, they are still may be responsible for one another's debts, depending on state laws.

We do not recommend separate bank accounts. Couples need to do what works for them, but in our experience, it is best that a couple join their money in a single account and then do the hard work of communicating a common approach to money and a specific plan for how that money is to be spent.

Our relationship with money, often unexplored, is usually forged out of the experience of the family in which we have been raised. We may have developed an attitude from our families that is totally unintended by our parents. Lori's father, raised in the Depression, could not pass up a sale on food items, even when he did not need the items!

Consequently, Lori has childhood memories of lots of cans of tuna and jars of mayonnaise stored in the basement because Dad never passed up a deal to buy "two cans for the price of one." Robert's parents, also raised in the Depression, went into debt every Christmas to give their sons the toys and clothes that they did not receive when they were children.

When you hear yourself or your spouse say, "I only want for my kids what I did not have," that is a clue that the real financial needs of your children are not what is driving your behavior as much as something deep within you. If you go into debt simply to give your kids what "you did not have," you may not really be meeting their needs as much as your unmet need from childhood. It is helpful to take a hard look at your relationship with money.

St. Paul actually has a wise piece of advice for money management:

Let no debt remain outstanding except the continuing debt to love one another... Romans 13:8 (NIV)

We have struggled over the years to actually write down a budget and track our expenses. But we have been able to follow this principal of "owing no debt..." The two items for which we have borrowed money have been house and car; that's it. Everything else is paid in cash or, if by a credit card, that balance is paid off in full at the end of each month.

"Money is hard to come by but easy to spend." What takes a month of work to acquire can be gone in an hour. With money we buy homes, pay for music lessons, pay taxes, give to charity, and buy gifts for Christmas. How we spend our money probably says more about who we are and what we value than anything else we do. Thus, it is most important that couples talk about money and come to some agreement over its meaning and use. Jesus says,

Therefore I tell you, do not worry about your life, what you will eat [or drink], or about your body, what you will wear...All these things the pagans seek. Your heavenly Father knows that you need them all. But seek first the kingdom (of God) and his righteousness, and all these things will be given you besides. Matthew 6:25-33

St. Paul says the "love" of money is the root of all evil. Money does matter, and Paul, in the same letter to Timothy (6:17-18), gives direction to the right use of money.

Tell the rich in the present age not to be proud and not to rely on so uncertain a thing as wealth but rather on God, who richly provides us with all things for our enjoyment. Tell them to do good, to be rich in good works, to be generous, ready to share, thus accumulating as treasure a good foundation for the future, so as to win the life that is true life.

Couple Exercise: *Review this article. What are some points that you agree with? Disagree with? Need to think about?*

Complete the Money Inventory separately, and then talk about it. Use My Turn/Your Turn as needed.

Money Inventory On a scale from 1-10 indicate your level of agreement with the following statements with a 10 = Yes, 5 = Sometimes, and a 1 = No.

	No			Sometimes					Yes	
1. We quarrel over money.	1	2	3	4	5	6	7	8	9	10
2. We are able to maintain a budget.	1	2	3	4	5	6	7	8	9	10
3. I am an effective money manager.	1	2	3	4	5	6	7	8	9	10
4. My spouse is an effective money manager.	1	2	3	4	5	6	7	8	9	10
5. We agree on how to balance work with family.	1	2	3	4	5	6	7	8	9	10
6. My spouse earns enough money.	1	2	3	4	5	6	7	8	9	10
7. I have enough money to spend on my personal needs, interests, and hobbies.	1	2	3	4	5	6	7	8	9	10
8. My spouse is a compulsive shopper.	1	2	3	4	5	6	7	8	9	10
9. I am a compulsive shopper.	1	2	3	4	5	6	7	8	9	10
10. The money is "our money," not his or hers.	1	2	3	4	5	6	7	8	9	10
11. Debt is not a problem in our marriage.	1	2	3	4	5	6	7	8	9	10
12. Material possessions are very important to me and my spouse.	1	2	3	4	5	6	7	8	9	10
13. We are able to save for long-term goals.	1	2	3	4	5	6	7	8	9	10
14. I trust my spouse with our money.	1	2	3	4	5	6	7	8	9	10
15. We share our money with people in need.	1	2	3	4	5	6	7	8	9	10
16. I would stay married to my spouse if we were poor.	1	2	3	4	5	6	7	8	9	10

What does money mean to you?

What does money mean to your spouse?

Complete the following sentences:
When I consider our financial situation and the role of money in our marriage I feel _____ because...

Something I think we ought to consider doing to bring greater unity between us in regards to money is...

CHAPTER 11

Holy Communion over a Lifetime

Holy Communion is a phrase most commonly used to refer to receiving the Eucharist, the sacramental body and blood of Jesus, during the celebration of the Lord's Supper. Catholics believe that when Jesus gives himself in the Eucharist, He does not hold back! Everything that makes Jesus who He is - body, soul, and divinity - is given to us in the consecrated bread and wine. Jesus does this in the same way that spouses do in marriage, without reservation, for the whole of His life with us, with the hope of creating new life in and through us.

Jesus' gift of Himself in the Eucharist creates communion with us. Catholics commonly call this exchange "Holy Communion." Spouses' gift of themselves to one another in marriage, especially through sexual intimacy, also creates a "holy communion," the joining together of wife and husband in married love. Marriage is not simply two physical bodies being joined together in "holy communion." In marriage two persons with personalities, hopes, dreams, fears, and free will, give the totality of themselves to one another in love. This happens in a myriad of ways from sharing chores, to raising children, to paying the bills, but it happens most profoundly through sexual intimacy.

Catholics understand marriage to be a Sacrament. This means that marriage as an institution does not originate with the Church, but with God. Sacraments are outward signs - something you can see, touch, or smell - that give grace. The outward sign of the Sacrament of the Eucharist is the consecrated bread and wine. One can see it, touch it, and taste it, and when it is consumed it becomes spiritual food that nourishes faith.

Marriage is a sacrament that reveals the gift of God's love for humanity. As husbands and wives love one another in a sacrificial way, their love serves as a reminder to the Church and society how God loves us in Jesus. Marriage forms an intimate communion of husband and wife, two bodies that become one flesh. The sacramental sign of marriage is sexual intimacy. When spouses join together in sexual intimacy they essentially become one physical body. This embrace points to a deeper communion that is happening in the relationship and, in fact, is the goal of marriage - the joining of heart and soul between wife and husband.

What the Eucharist is to the Church - Holy Communion, sexual intimacy is to marriage - also a Holy Communion.

St. Paul describes what communion looks like in his letter to the Philippians.

If there is any encouragement in Christ, any solace in love, any participation in the Spirit, any compassion and mercy, complete my joy by being of the same mind, with the same love, united in heart, thinking one thing. Philippians 2:1-2

Paul is merely echoing Jesus' sentiments as a good Jew.

Some Pharisees approached him, and tested him, saying, "Is it lawful for a man to divorce his wife for any cause whatever?" He said in reply, "Have you not read that from the beginning the Creator 'made them male and female' and said, 'For this reason a man shall leave his father and mother and be joined to his wife and the two shall become one flesh.' So they are no longer two, but one flesh. Therefore, what God has joined together no human being must separate." Matthew 19:3-6

Marriage brings two very different people together and forges them into a "holy communion," a joining of minds and hearts. What happens sacramentally on the wedding day, the uniting of two individuals into "one body", takes a lifetime to complete psychologically, emotionally, and spiritually.

"Holy Communion" in marriage mirrors and participates in the "Holy Communion" that exists within God. The Trinity is the great mystery of God's self-giving love between the Father and the Son through the Holy Spirit. In this mystery there is no domination, no oppression, and no suppression of the other. The Father, Son, and Spirit are full persons, fully united in the free gift of self, one to the other. This is the goal of marriage. When authentic communion is present, each spouse is fully free to be him or herself. And when couples desire this communion, and work at it on a daily basis, they become Sacraments not simply of God's love for humanity as St. Paul writes about in Ephesians (5:25), but of God's very nature of self-giving love within the Trinity.[34]

One of the most beautiful descriptions of communion in marriage that we have found is in a novel written by Louis de Bernieres called <u>Corelli's Mandolin</u>. The context of this short discussion on marriage is that the Italian army has occupied a small Greek island during World War II. Greek families are forced to lodge Italian officers. Dr. Iannis and his daughter Pelagia have taken in the Italian Captain Corelli, and the father decides it is time that he has a "heart-to-heart" talk with his daughter over "the Captain."

"It has not escaped my notice, Pelagia, that you have fallen in love with the captain."

She flushed violently, looked perfectly horrified, and began to stammer. "The captain?" she repeated foolishly.

"Yes, the captain, our uninvited but charming guest. He who plays the mandolin in the moonlight and brings you Italian confectionery that you do not always see fit to share with your father. This latter being the one whom you presume to be both blind and stupid."

"Papakis," she protested, too taken aback to add any kind of articulate coda to this intervention...

The doctor waved his pipe expansively. "Really, this point is not worth denying or discussing, because it is all very obvious. The diagnosis has been made and confirmed. We should be discussing the implications. By the way, it is clear to me that he also is in love with you..."

"Technically the captain is an enemy. Can you conceive the torment that would be inflicted upon you by others when they judge that you have renounced the love of a patriotic Greek, in favor of an invader, an oppressor?...You would have to move away to Italy if you wanted to stay with him because here you might not be safe..."

"And another thing. Love is a temporary madness, it erupts like volcanoes and then subsides. And when it subsides you have to make a decision. You have to work out whether your roots have so entwined together that it is inconceivable that you should ever part. Because this is what love is. Love is not breathlessness, it is not excitement, it is not the promulgation of promises of eternal passion, it is not the desire to mate every second minute of the day, it is not lying awake at night imagining that he is kissing every cranny of your body. No, don't blush, I am telling you some truths. That is just being "in love," which any fool can do. Love itself is what is left over when being in love has burned away, and this is both an art and a fortunate accident. Your mother and I had it, we had roots that drew towards each other underground, and when all the pretty blossoms had fallen from our branches we found that we were one tree and not two."

"But sometimes the petals fall away and the roots have not entwined. Imagine giving up your home and your people, only to discover after six months, a year, three years, that the trees have had no roots and have fallen over. Imagine the desolation. Imagine the imprisonment." pp. 279-281.

The seeds of communion are planted when couples become engaged, and blossom into a small plant on their wedding day, but it takes a lifetime for this communion to grow into full bloom, and the two roots to intertwine into one.

Couple Exercise: *Review the above reflection on communion. Comment on anything that stands out for you.*

Consider your life together; when have you felt most united to one another? What were the events and circumstances, and who were the people that helped make this happen?

Communion and Decision-Making Communion is a choice; it does not "just happen."

> ***Our Story by Robert*** *We were slow learners when it came to problem-solving in a way that maintained communion. We unconsciously thought that the goal of decision-making was to "get my way" which then meant we argued a lot trying to persuade the other to "my" point of view.*
>
> *It was not until we had been married about 10 years and faced a major decision that a priest friend reminded us that the goal of marriage is "communion." The issue at hand was that I wanted to move the family back to Seattle after we had been in Yakima a couple of years. We met with my spiritual director who said, "As you look for what you are to do in this particular issue, begin your conversation with where you have unity." Duh!*
>
> *Lori, in fact, had no energy for such a move at this time. Since this was an issue for me, but not one for her, I was able to let it go for the sake of communion.*

Problem-Solving and Decision-Making If your goal is "communion," begin your problem-solving and decision-making with where you have agreement. Here is a method to help you do that, but keep in mind that agreement means either:

a) we both like the idea or decision at hand, or

b) one or the other may not like it, but can live with it.

> **IMPORTANT:** Never do something that your spouse has said she or he cannot live with! Should such an issue come up, then couples need to keep talking until they find a way that is acceptable to both spouses, or they drop it.

1. Write down the issue(s) to be discussed.

2. Have a conversation to listen to one another without trying to solve the issue.

3. Brainstorm solutions. Each takes a sheet of paper and writes down eight-ten ways you could work on the issue at hand. BE AS SPECIFIC AS YOU CAN BE! Write down even those ideas that seem outlandish. This is "thinking outside-the-box" time!

4. Compare your answers. (**This is important.**)

   A. Place a check next to any idea that you or your spouse wrote that you really like.

   B. Place a question mark next to any idea that you or your spouse wrote that you do not really like, but you could live with.

   C. Place an underline{X} next to any idea that you or your spouse wrote that you do not like, and could not live with.

**If you have any questions about your spouse's ideas, simply ask her/him to help you understand what this means.

5. Transfer the answers to the worksheet provided.

6. Columns A and B show you where you have agreement in your problem solving solutions. Begin your

problem-solving conversation here. Select any or all that you want to do.

7. Discard column C, unless there is an item there that is very important to one of you. Use the speaker-listener method and X, Y, Z statements to discuss it. Then use the above method to see if you can find any common ground on how to include it.

Couple Exercise I: Now practice this method with this issue: Identify three-five ways that you can work on your marriage.

Couple Exercise II – Repeat this activity. This time select an issue that has come up through reading this book. Follow the above process, but before you do so, pray this prayer:

O loving God, thank you for our marriage! Thank you for all the love, work, fun, and even conflict of our "holy communion." Be with us as we search out what to do with this issue—(name the issue). Guide us towards a decision that will keep us united with each other in faith, hope, and love. We ask this in the name of Jesus. Amen.

Protecting Our Holy Communion Worksheet (Copy this page for future use.)

1. Define the problem. _____

   _____

2. On separate sheets of paper, brainstorm solutions.

3. Compare answers; place a <u>checkmark</u> next to those that you like, a <u>question mark</u> next to those that you do not like, but could live with, and an <u>X</u> next to those that you cannot live with.

4. Transfer the answers to the columns below.

5. Discuss the answers in columns A and B; discard column C. Use the X, Y, Z statements and speaker-listener method as needed.

a. We both like it!	b. One of us does not like it, but can live with it!	c. One of us cannot live with it. (These you discard)

6. Your decision is:

7. Your timeframe for re-looking at the issue is:

8. Date, time, and place when you will meet to evaluate how things are going:

CHAPTER 12

Your Future Together

When young people fall in love and decide to marry they do so with no idea of what a lifetime together really means. We certainly did not. We were in love, and being together was everything. When we thought about the future, we imagined it filled with children, family, and friends, and problem-free.

Life has a way of coming along and popping romantic illusions and preparing newlyweds for the long-haul. Our "long haul" began in 1978, and as we consider our future together today, there are three primary lessons that we have learned that help sharpen our commitment to each other:

1) Life is short.
2) Life brings many surprises.
3) We will suffer in life.

Life is short. Rob's parents, Tony and Evelyn had been married 39 years when he died at the young age of 61. Evelyn lived for another 20 years. She had no idea that when she first said, "I do," on June 27, 1949, she would outlive her husband by 20 years. She hated being a widow but never remarried.

Lori's parents, John and Paula were married for 53 years before John died in 2006 of various complications with his health, including heart failure. Paula misses him every day, but she is in good health and lives near family and friends.

Our good friend Lynn's husband died after 10 years of marriage from brain cancer. Bette's husband died after 25 years of marriage, also from cancer. Our dear friend Diane died when the car her husband was driving skidded off the road on an icy winter night and hit a pole. Dennis was left alone to raise their five young children.

Life is short. You do not know how many years you will have together. Hang on to each other and keep your communion intact.

Life will bring you many surprises. We planned on Rob's going to graduate school after his graduation from LSU, but Lori got pregnant and had a baby two months after his graduation. He delayed graduate school and went right into the work force. Babies came faster than we thought they would, three children in four years. But, surprise, Rob was offered a scholarship for graduate school, so we did something we never imagined, took it and moved away from both of our families to Maryland where the school was located.

On three separate occasions we took in teenagers who were having serious problems at home, and a brother who was recovering from a divorce. None of this was part of our long-range plans, but happened quickly and spontaneously because of the pressing need. This was a big adjustment for our children who had to make room for our guests who were welcomed as members of the family.

Life surprises are common to everyone. John lost his business when the economy tanked. Bob was hit by a car while riding his bike home from work. Paula, with children at home, needed to return to work when her husband's business was struggling. Jim was denied a military promotion, one he was confident he would receive. Rena's daughter ran off with her boyfriend to marry in Las Vegas. Sally's son was kicked out of school for drug use. Laura's son was diagnosed with Asberger's Syndrome.

Life brings daily surprises, many good, many that make little difference, and many that bring great challenges to married love. There is a Scripture passage that we have come to rely on and helps us to trust in God's providential care when life's surprises show up:

We know that all things work for good for those who love God, who are called according to his purpose.
Romans 8:28

You do not know what surprises life will bring you. But get prepared, because come they will.

You will suffer in life. There is no way around this. Life, even at its best, brings suffering. We moved away from south Louisiana where Rob's parents, Tony and Evelyn, lived so that Rob could go to graduate school in Maryland. The year we moved was the year Tony retired from teaching. He adored his grandchildren, Steven, Clare, and Mary, and loved coming by the house to pick them up and take them to get ice cream. The timing of our move was terrible, and we know it brought Tony and Evelyn great heartache to be separated from their grandchildren.

We've already told you the story of how Tony and Evelyn lived with her bi-polar disorder. There was no clear-cut path for her healing and no way of anticipating when depression would rear its ugly head. No one in the family had any experience with mental illness, and it presented quite a challenge to all family members to care for her.

We do not get to choose <u>if</u> we will suffer, but we do get some say in <u>how</u> we will suffer. We can suffer in a way that leads to life or we can suffer in a way that leads to death. Wisdom is in learning the difference.

Women in childbirth suffer in a way that is life-giving. This is an obvious example, but others also suffer for positive ends: students, athletes, musicians, and workers who discipline their minds and bodies in order to achieve a certain goal. Persons who struggle with addiction suffer one way when they keep up the habit, and another way when they check themselves into a treatment center to resolve it.

Couples that are struggling with trust and betrayal, as did John and Jane Doe, can choose to go to counseling and do the slow, difficult work of learning to rebuild trust. This certainly involves a type of suffering in facing the shame, acts of betrayal, and issues that led to the break in the relationship, and then learning the skills and developing the trust to restore things. This kind of suffering leads to forgiveness and life.

Divorce <u>may</u> be a necessary option; but for too many couples in trouble it is often the easiest option, too quickly acted upon. It is easier to give in to the anger and bitterness, and war against a spouse than to work on learning how to be successful in marriage. Keep in mind, if there are children involved, the divorce does not settle the battles (and suffering) that will continue as ex-spouses negotiate their care.

We know of three marriages that were restored because the wives, against all reason, forgave their husbands who had abandoned them and the children, then returned seeking forgiveness. Two of these marriages had ended in divorce, but the husbands came back, and, after months of marriage counseling, the couples reconciled. One husband also needed mental health counseling and medication to help manage some of his compulsions, but all three couples are now married, and happily so.

Certainly some marriages cannot be saved and should not be, especially where abuse and/or substance abuse are present. However, research shows that, if a couple is struggling with their marriage and they hang in there, and suffer through the work it takes to make things better, the marriage does get better. *"Eighty-six percent of unhappily married people who stick it out find that, five years later, their marriages are happier ... Permanent marital unhappiness is surprisingly rare among the couples who stick it out."*[35]

You will suffer in life—that is a given. But how you suffer is a choice. Choose the suffering that leads to life.

Your Future Together Life is short; there are many surprises; suffering happens. And yet God's Kingdom is deeply present in the midst of these realities, especially in your life-long covenant of love to be true to one another in good times and in bad, in sickness and health, in poverty or wealth, till death do you part.

Couples Activity – *Complete the Future Inventory separately, then compare your answers. Use My Turn/Your Turn as necessary.*

The Future Inventory On a scale from 1-10 indicate your level of agreement with the following statements with a 10 = Yes, 5 = Sometimes, and a 1 = No.

	No				Sometimes					Yes
1. We agree on long-term goals for our future.	1	2	3	4	5	6	7	8	9	10
2. We are satisfied with our preparations for when we retire.	1	2	3	4	5	6	7	8	9	10
3. We are living where we want to live.	1	2	3	4	5	6	7	8	9	10
4. The working spouse(s) is happy with her/his job.	1	2	3	4	5	6	7	8	9	10
5. We have prayed about God's will for our future.	1	2	3	4	5	6	7	8	9	10
6. We have advance directives in the event that illness will leave one of us on life support.	1	2	3	4	5	6	7	8	9	10
7. I am satisfied with where our children are at this stage of their lives.	1	2	3	4	5	6	7	8	9	10
8. I am not worried about spending more time with my spouse during retirement.	1	2	3	4	5	6	7	8	9	10
9. We have discussed giving more time to serving the poor and elderly.	1	2	3	4	5	6	7	8	9	10
10. We have a list of things we would like to do before we die.	1	2	3	4	5	6	7	8	9	10
11. I am at peace with God and my church.	1	2	3	4	5	6	7	8	9	10
12. My spouse is at peace with God and his/her church.	1	2	3	4	5	6	7	8	9	10
13. There are no family relationships that are strained and need attention.	1	2	3	4	5	6	7	8	9	10
14. We are comfortable with our efforts to care for our aging parents.	1	2	3	4	5	6	7	8	9	10
15. Our burial plans are complete.	1	2	3	4	5	6	7	8	9	10

When I consider our long-term future together, I feel
_____ because...

CHAPTER 13

Epilogue - Marriage and the Kingdom of God

Your marriage is not just for you and your children. It is part of God's plan to give you a strong foundation from which to go into the world of your daily life and be a power for good.

You are the salt of the earth. But if salt loses its taste, with what can it be seasoned? It is no longer good for anything but to be thrown out and trampled underfoot.

You are the light of the world. A city set on a mountain cannot be hidden. Nor do they light a lamp and then put it under a bushel basket; it is set on a lampstand, where it gives light to all in the house.

Just so, your light must shine before others, that they may see your good deeds and glorify your heavenly Father. (Matthew 5:13-16)

Jesus preached a kingdom that he believed was breaking into human history. He did not just gather together disciples, teach the Beatitudes, heal the sick, drive out demons, eat with the social outcasts, pray alone and with others, and confront the hypocrisy of the religious leaders to get you and me to heaven after our deaths. For Jesus, human life this side of eternity had purpose. He prayed that God's will be done on earth as it is done in heaven, and not only taught his disciples to pray the same, but "to do" the same: to work for the coming of the Kingdom.

The "Kingdom of God" is nothing less than the Holy Spirit fully alive and active in creation: working for love to overcome hate, hope to conquer despair, and faith to be victorious over sin and suffering. The Kingdom of God is vast and present in creation and among all people who sincerely seek God and strive to be guided by love.

For Christians, Jesus is the fullest manifestation of the Kingdom of God in history. And the Church universal is a sacrament of the Kingdom of God revealed in Jesus. The Church exists for one purpose, to make the Kingdom of God, revealed by Jesus, present to every generation in history, until Jesus comes again in glory.

Christian marriage is a sacrament of the Kingdom of God through the Church. It is a visible and tangible institution that God uses to build strong individuals, families, neighborhoods, schools — the building blocks for a good and just society. Every marriage creates a "domestic Church" where faith in Jesus is learned, lived, shared, and celebrated.

- *From your marriage your children should meet Christ;*

- *from your marriage the poor should meet Christ;*

- *from your marriage your neighbors should meet Christ;*

- *from your marriage your colleagues at work should meet Christ;*

- *and from your marriage you and your spouse should meet Christ.*

Marriages that serve the Kingdom of God are sacrificial marriages. Communication skills are necessary, and shared values and goals are all important, but a couple who wants to have a long and happy future together, a future until "death do us part," must learn to sacrifice for the good of the marriage. Sacrifice looks different for different couples. It essentially involves two things:

Saying "No!" to any person, place, thing, future plans, or past regrets that get in the way of the relationship (and very often this means "No" to positive and good things like work, time at church, outings with friends, working at a hobby, or watching television);

And "Yes!" to whatever maintains and enhances your holy communion.

You have discovered the "treasure hidden in a field, and the pearl of great price" and with it have gained enormous benefits that no amount of money could buy! Through your marriage:

• *You work as a team.*

• *You discover your gifts individually and as a couple, and put them to use in your family and in the world around you.*

• *You work hard at being good stewards with your money, and good neighbors and citizens.*

• *You go to your jobs with the goal of doing your best so that you can make a difference in the world while providing for your family.*

• *You take time for fun and sexual intimacy.*

• *You forgive each other as God has forgiven you.*

• *You welcome children and raise them to love God and to love their neighbor as they love themselves.*

• *If you cannot have children, you find other ways to be generous and give of yourselves in unselfish service.*

• *And when you get sick, tired, and discouraged, you turn to one another for care and comfort.*

You have heeded the wisdom of Jesus to build your house on rock.

Everyone who listens to these words of mine and acts on them will be like a wise man who built his house on rock. The rain fell, the floods came, and the winds blew and buffeted the house. But it did not collapse; it had been set solidly on rock. And everyone who listens to these words of mine but does not act on them will be like a fool who built his house on sand. The rain fell, the floods came, and the winds blew and buffeted the house, and it collapsed and was completely ruined." (Mt 7:24-28)

Through your marriage, you have created a foundation of life and love that will last a lifetime. It is hard! It is demanding! But the best and most amazing gift you will ever give your children, neighbors, community, church and country, and especially each other, is your marriage.

Your marriage is truly an amazing gift, a wonderful treasure that is no longer hidden but open to everyone around you, enriching them by your love.

Couple Exercise:

1. Review the previous article. Underline any points that stand out for you.

2. What do these points say to you in your marriage?

Marriage Success - An Assessment: (Circle one answer from the multiple choice options.)

Teamwork

1 A.   We work together as a team.
       1) always   2) often   3) sometimes   4) never

1 B   We know how to tackle a project together and successfully complete it.
       1) always   2) often   3) sometimes   4) never

A good memory I have of our learning to work as a team is...

Self-Discovery

2 A.   My spouse is very gifted and uses his/her gifts to enrich our family.
       1) always   2) often   3) sometimes   4) never

2 B.   My spouse is very aware of my gifts and encourages me to use them to enrich our family.
       1) always   2) often   3) sometimes   4) never

A good memory I have of each of us using our gifts for the good of the family is...

Maturity

3 A.   Marriage brings out the best in me.
       1) always   2) often   3) sometimes   4) never

3 B.   I can look back on my marriage and see how through it I have become a better person.
       1) always   2) often   3) sometimes   4) never

A good memory I have of our marriage helping me grow as a person is...

Wealth-Building

4 A.   I am satisfied that we have the money we need to live the lifestyle we want to live.
       1) always   2) often   3) sometimes   4) never

4 B.   We agree on our approach to money, how we are to save, spend, and give a portion of it to charity.
       1) always   2) often   3) sometimes   4) never

A good memory that I have when we made a good choice related to money is...

Healthy Lifestyles

5 A.   We are committed to and work at living a healthy lifestyle, including nurturing a spiritual life.
       1) always   2) often   3) sometimes   4) never

5 B.   We have a healthy balance of work, leisure time, nutritious diet, exercise, spirituality, and sleep.
1) always   2) often   3) sometimes   4) never

A good memory that I have of our living a balanced life is...

Workplace Success

6 A.   My relationships at work (or home for the homemaker) are very positive and productive.
1) always   2) often   3) sometimes   4) never

6 B.   I am confident at what I do, and receive affirmation and encouragement for it.
1) always   2) often   3) sometimes   4) never

A good memory that I have when I truly enjoyed my work and/or being a homemaker is....

Best Caregiver

7 A.   My spouse takes good care of me when I am not feeling well.
1) always   2) often   3) sometimes   4) never

7 B.   My spouse is the first person that I turned to for care when I am not feeling well.
1) always   2) often   3) sometimes   4) never

A good memory that I have of my spouse's caring for me when I was not feeling well is...

Good Neighbors

8 A.   It is very important to us to be good neighbors and pay attention to what is going on in the community.
1) always   2) often   3) sometimes   4) never

8 B.   We are active in helping our neighborhood and community become a better place to live.
1) always   2) often   3) sometimes   4) never

A good memory that I have of our family reaching out to neighbors is...

Friends

9 A.   My spouse and I are the best of friends; I can fully be myself with my spouse.
1) always   2) often   3) sometimes   4) never

9 B.   We regularly make time for fun and leisure.
1) always   2) often   3) sometimes   4) never

A good memory that I have of us being friends is...

FOR THOSE WITH CHILDREN

10 A.   Our children wonderfully enrich our marriage.
   1) always   2) often   3) sometimes   4) never

10 B. Being parents has brought my spouse and me closer together.
   1) always   2) often   3) sometimes   4) never

A good memory that I have of our being with our children is...

Mental Health

11 A.   We are very good at dealing with conflict.
   1) always   2) often   3) sometimes   4) never

11 B.   We are careful not to hurt one another with our words or actions during a conflict.
   1) always   2) often   3) sometimes   4) never

A good memory that I have of our effectively dealing with a serious problem is...

Great Sex

12 A.   I am satisfied with our sexual life and find it pleasurable, meaningful, and frequent enough.
   1) always   2) often   3) sometimes   4) never

   B.   As we get older we are able to speak with each other about our changing needs related to sex.
   1) always   2) often   3) sometimes   4) never

A good memory that I have of a very satisfying sexual encounter with my spouse is...

Tally your score. Count the number of 1's, 2's, 3's, and 4's you circled. Write down each tally, then multiply that number by the indicated factor (e.g. If you had eight 1s, the score would be 8 x 1 = 8. If you had eight 2s, the score would be 8 x 2 =16). Add the sums together to determine your total score. **The lower the score, the more successful the marriage**.

With children:
24 to 37 = Very Successful Marriage;
38 to 61 = Successful Marriage;
62 to 86 = Marriage Needs Attention;
87 or greater = HELP!

Without children:
22 to 33 = Very Successful Marriage;
34 to 55 = Successful Marriage;
56 to 76 = Marriage Needs Attention;
77 or greater = HELP!

Example:

Number of 1's: 5 x 1 = 5
Number of 2's: 12 x 2 = 24
Number of 3's: 5 x 3 = 15
Number of 4's: 4 x 1 = 4
              Total = 48

Your score:

Number of 1's: _____ x 1 = _____
Number of 2's: _____ x 2 = _____
Number of 3's: _____ x 3 = _____
Number of 4's: _____ x 4 = _____

            Total = _____

Reflection Questions:

1. List all the categories where you gave yourself ones or twos.

2. List all the categories where you gave yourself threes or fours.

3. Complete this sentence: When I consider how successful we are in our marriage I feel _____
*   because…*

4. Some things that I need to do to make our marriage stronger are…

5. Some things that I need from my spouse to make our marriage stronger are…

Why I Married: An Assessment — *Indicate your agreement with each statement by circling one of the four words beneath each statement that most corresponds to why you married. Complete separately and compare your answers. Use My Turn/Your Turn as needed.*

1. My fiancé had good connections and I thought this marriage would help me get ahead in life.
   Absolutely   Somewhat   Not Really   No

2. My fiancé had money and a knack for making money, and together we could live a lifestyle that required large incomes.
   Absolutely   Somewhat   Not Really   No

3. Marriage was the ticket out of my home and family, which was not a good place to be.
   Absolutely   Somewhat   Not Really   No

4. We sort of slipped into marriage after realizing we liked being together.
   Absolutely   Somewhat   Not Really   No

5. I was passionately in love and marriage seemed to be the logical next step.
   Absolutely   Somewhat   Not Really   No

6. I knew that this was the person that I wanted to be the other parent of my children.
   Absolutely   Somewhat   Not Really   No

7. The sex was great. Why not get married?
   Absolutely   Somewhat   Not Really   No

8. Our friends were all getting married, and it seemed like a good idea for us to do so.
   Absolutely   Somewhat   Not Really   No

9. I felt pressure from my family to find a suitable spouse who had career goals and was attractive.
   Absolutely   Somewhat   Not Really   No

10. We both sensed that God was calling us to marriage, and we could not wait to have kids.
    Absolutely   Somewhat   Not Really   No

11. Other. Is there a reason that you married that is not part of this list? If so, what is it?

Power of Words Inventory On a scale from 1 to 10 indicate your level of agreement with the following statements with a 10 = Yes, 5 = Sometimes, and a 1 = No.

	No				Sometimes					Yes
1. My spouse orders me around and tells me what to do.	1	2	3	4	5	6	7	8	9	10
2. My spouse threatens me with consequences.	1	2	3	4	5	6	7	8	9	10
3. My spouse tells me what I should and should not do, and tries to persuade me through guilt.	1	2	3	4	5	6	7	8	9	10
4. My spouse gives me solutions and advice when I try to talk to him/her.	1	2	3	4	5	6	7	8	9	10
5. My spouse lectures and tries to persuade me with facts and figures.	1	2	3	4	5	6	7	8	9	10
6. My spouse interrogates and digs for information.	1	2	3	4	5	6	7	8	9	10
7. My spouse analyzes my motives and behaviors and has figured out what I think before I do.	1	2	3	4	5	6	7	8	9	10
8. My spouse criticizes, judges, and blames.	1	2	3	4	5	6	7	8	9	10
9. My spouse ridicules, calls me names, and uses sarcasm.	1	2	3	4	5	6	7	8	9	10
10. My spouse manipulates by saying what I want to hear, but does not tell me the full truth.	1	2	3	4	5	6	7	8	9	10
11. My spouse disregards my feelings and emotions through humor and jokes.	1	2	3	4	5	6	7	8	9	10
12. My spouse withdraws through silence and/or busyness.	1	2	3	4	5	6	7	8	9	10

Reflection Questions:

1. When my spouse speaks to me using any of the above negative ways of communication I feel _____ _____ because…

2. When I look at the above list, I am guilty of doing numbers…

Interpersonal Inventory Spouses have certain interpersonal needs that they agree will be met exclusively through one another. The challenge is to become aware of these needs and communicate them in healthy ways. On a scale from 1-10 indicate your level of agreement with the following statements with a 10 = Yes, 5 = Sometimes, and a 1 = No.

	No				Sometimes					Yes
18. I trust my spouse when he/she is away.	1	2	3	4	5	6	7	8	9	10
19. I make time to talk on a regular basis.	1	2	3	4	5	6	7	8	9	10
20. My spouse listens to me.	1	2	3	4	5	6	7	8	9	10
21. I can be fully myself with my spouse.	1	2	3	4	5	6	7	8	9	10
22. My spouse does not try to change me.	1	2	3	4	5	6	7	8	9	10
23. My spouse is affectionate.	1	2	3	4	5	6	7	8	9	10
24. My spouse is kind.	1	2	3	4	5	6	7	8	9	10
25. I like my spouse's family.	1	2	3	4	5	6	7	8	9	10
26. My spouse acts in my best interest.	1	2	3	4	5	6	7	8	9	10
27. My spouse never takes me for granted.	1	2	3	4	5	6	7	8	9	10
28. My spouse enjoys my friends.	1	2	3	4	5	6	7	8	9	10
29. My spouse understands me better than anyone.	1	2	3	4	5	6	7	8	9	10
30. I feel safe with my spouse.	1	2	3	4	5	6	7	8	9	10
31. My spouse isn't very controlling.	1	2	3	4	5	6	7	8	9	10
32. My spouse shares his/her feelings.	1	2	3	4	5	6	7	8	9	10
33. My spouse shows me lots of appreciation.	1	2	3	4	5	6	7	8	9	10
34. I admire my spouse.	1	2	3	4	5	6	7	8	9	10

When I consider how different we are from each other and the basic needs that I have for trust, friendship, fun, intimacy, acceptance, and appreciation, I feel _____ because…

Something that I think we need to do to better meet one another's interpersonal needs is

Discovering How I Prefer to Give and Receive Love (See *The Five Love Languages,* by Gary Chapman, for a more thorough exercise to discover your Love Language). There are 10 pairs of sentences below. Each one states how a person likes to be loved and cared for. Compare the sentences in a set and indicate your preference in each pair by marking a check in the space provided. Compile your answers using the chart below.

1 _____ I feel so good when you send me flowers. (B)
_____ I like it when you give me hugs. (A)

2. _____ I am grateful when you bring me a new DVD. (B)
_____ I enjoy playing a board game with you. (C)

3. _____ I love it when you say, "Thank you." (D)
_____ It is fun riding bikes with you. (C)

4. _____ I need to hear you speak kindly even on difficult topics. (D)
_____ I really appreciate it when you prepare a snack for me. (E)

5. _____ It is so great to sit next to you and feel your body next to mine. (A)
_____ I like taking a walk with you. (C)

6. _____ A back rub feels really good. (A)
_____ I appreciate it when you give me a compliment. (D)

7. _____ I love to read and enjoy getting a book. (B)
_____ I am grateful when you do your share of the work around home. (E)

8. _____ I like holding hands with you. (A)
_____ I appreciate it when you run errands for me. (E)

9. _____ I get so excited when you give me a music CD. (B)
_____ I sure like being encouraged by positive words from you. (D)

10. _____ I like to have time to sit and be together. (C)
_____ I am grateful when you help me to succeed at my commitments. (E)

Add up the **Totals** number of the letters that you selected and place them in the column to the right.

A___ Touch

B___ Gifts

C___ Quality Time

D___ Kind Words

E___ Service

Your Love language is…

Reflection question: I feel most loved by you when you do _____ because…

Friendship Inventory On a scale from 1-10 indicate your level of agreement with the following statements with a 10 = Yes, 5 = Sometimes, and a 1 = No.

	No				Sometimes					Yes
1. We have many common interests.	1	2	3	4	5	6	7	8	9	10
2. I'm okay with the leisure time my spouse spends separate from me.	1	2	3	4	5	6	7	8	9	10
3. We can afford my spouse's leisure activities.	1	2	3	4	5	6	7	8	9	10
4. We often do fun things together.	1	2	3	4	5	6	7	8	9	10
5. My spouse spends too much time with friends.	1	2	3	4	5	6	7	8	9	10
6. My spouse spends too much time with hobbies.	1	2	3	4	5	6	7	8	9	10
7. I tell my spouse everything.	1	2	3	4	5	6	7	8	9	10
8. My spouse tells me everything.	1	2	3	4	5	6	7	8	9	10
9. I trust my spouse to keep intimate matters private.	1	2	3	4	5	6	7	8	9	10
10. I can count on my spouse during difficult times.	1	2	3	4	5	6	7	8	9	10
11. My spouse spends too much time watching T.V.	1	2	3	4	5	6	7	8	9	10
12. My spouse spends too much time with electronic stuff from the cell phone to computer.	1	2	3	4	5	6	7	8	9	10
13. We date on a regular basis.	1	2	3	4	5	6	7	8	9	10
14. I can be myself with my spouse.	1	2	3	4	5	6	7	8	9	10

What are four activities that we do together for fun?
1.
2.
3.
4.
What fun activities do we do separately?
1. He:
2. She:
3. He:
4. She:

When I think about how we relate to one another as friends I feel _____ because:

Some things I think we could do to strengthen our friendship are:
1.
2.
3.

Children Inventory (includes blended family) On a scale from 1-10 indicate your level of agreement with the following statements with a 10 = Yes, 5 = Sometimes, and a 1 = No.

	No				Sometimes					Yes
1. I had a happy childhood.	1	2	3	4	5	6	7	8	9	10
2. My spouse had a happy childhood.	1	2	3	4	5	6	7	8	9	10
3. We agree on a method of family planning.	1	2	3	4	5	6	7	8	9	10
4. We agree on how to raise our children.	1	2	3	4	5	6	7	8	9	10
5. We argue about our children.	1	2	3	4	5	6	7	8	9	10
6. I think my spouse spends enough time with our children.	1	2	3	4	5	6	7	8	9	10
7. We agree on methods of discipline.	1	2	3	4	5	6	7	8	9	10
8. [If your children are teens or young adults] We agree on how to help them to mature.	1	2	3	4	5	6	7	8	9	10
9. I argue with our children.	1	2	3	4	5	6	7	8	9	10
10. We agree on the role of mother.	1	2	3	4	5	6	7	8	9	10
11. We agree on the role of the father.	1	2	3	4	5	6	7	8	9	10
12. I enjoy being with our children.	1	2	3	4	5	6	7	8	9	10
13. Raising children helps me grow as a person.	1	2	3	4	5	6	7	8	9	10
14. I am satisfied with the relationship I have with our children now.	1	2	3	4	5	6	7	8	9	10
15. I know our children's gifts.	1	2	3	4	5	6	7	8	9	10

Blended Families

	No				Sometimes					Yes
16. My stepchildren love and respect me.	1	2	3	4	5	6	7	8	9	10
17. Our two families are blending peacefully.	1	2	3	4	5	6	7	8	9	10

Complete the following sentences: *When I look back and consider our life with our children, I feel* _____ *because...*

When I consider our relationship with our children now, I feel _____ *because...*

Children Inventory (couples <u>without</u> children) On a scale from 1-10 indicate your level of agreement with the following statements with a 10 = Yes, 5 = Sometimes, and a 1 = No.

	No				Sometimes					Yes
	1	2	3	4	5	6	7	8	9	10
1. I had a happy childhood.	1	2	3	4	5	6	7	8	9	10
2. I was loved and accepted as a child.	1	2	3	4	5	6	7	8	9	10
3. My spouse had a happy childhood.	1	2	3	4	5	6	7	8	9	10
4. My spouse was loved and accepted as a child.	1	2	3	4	5	6	7	8	9	10
5. I enjoy being with children.	1	2	3	4	5	6	7	8	9	10
6. I love my nieces and nephews.	1	2	3	4	5	6	7	8	9	10
7. I enjoy my friends' children and often offer to baby-sit.	1	2	3	4	5	6	7	8	9	10
8. I have come to terms with the reasons we do not have children.	1	2	3	4	5	6	7	8	9	10
9. My spouse has come to terms with the reasons we do not have children.	1	2	3	4	5	6	7	8	9	10
10. Our parents and friends have come to terms with our not having children.	1	2	3	4	5	6	7	8	9	10
11. We enjoy helping other people and do so as a couple.	1	2	3	4	5	6	7	8	9	10
12. We are looking forward to growing old together as a couple.	1	2	3	4	5	6	7	8	9	10
13. I have lots of different interests that help me to fully enjoy life.	1	2	3	4	5	6	7	8	9	10
14. I am happy and at peace with where I am in life.	1	2	3	4	5	6	7	8	9	10

Complete the following sentences: *When I look back and consider our life without children, I feel* _____ *because...*

When I consider our relationship now and think about how we have been a "gift" to others,

I feel _____ *because...*

Children Inventory (newly married) On a scale from 1-10 indicate your level of agreement with the following statements with a 10 = Yes, 5 = Sometimes, and a 1 = No

	No				Sometimes					Yes
1. I was loved and accepted as a child.	1	2	3	4	5	6	7	8	9	10
2. I have good memories from childhood.	1	2	3	4	5	6	7	8	9	10
3. I liked how my parents raised me and want to do with our children what they did with me.	1	2	3	4	5	6	7	8	9	10
4. My spouse was loved as a child.	1	2	3	4	5	6	7	8	9	10
5. My spouse has good memories of his/her childhood.	1	2	3	4	5	6	7	8	9	10
6. I enjoy being with children.	1	2	3	4	5	6	7	8	9	10
7. My spouse wants to have children.	1	2	3	4	5	6	7	8	9	10
8. My spouse looks forward to becoming a parent.	1	2	3	4	5	6	7	8	9	10
9. We've discussed any fears or concerns about having children.	1	2	3	4	5	6	7	8	9	10
10. We agree on the number of children we would like to have.	1	2	3	4	5	6	7	8	9	10
11. Both families will be a great help in raising children.	1	2	3	4	5	6	7	8	9	10
12. We've carefully considered the merits of using Natural Family Planning.	1	2	3	4	5	6	7	8	9	10
13. We agree on how we will balance work with child-rearing.	1	2	3	4	5	6	7	8	9	10
14. My spouse liked how she/he was raised, and wants to parent like her/his parents.	1	2	3	4	5	6	7	8	9	10
15. We have good friends who will support us as parents.	1	2	3	4	5	6	7	8	9	10

Complete the following sentences: *When I consider the possibility of having children with my spouse some day, I feel _____ because…*

One thing we can do now to prepare ourselves to be successful parents is …

Faith and Community Inventory On a scale from 1-10 indicate your level of agreement with the following statements with a 10 = Yes, 5 = Sometimes, and a 1 = No.

	No				Sometimes					Yes
1. I have a personal relationship with Jesus.	1	2	3	4	5	6	7	8	9	10
2. Divorce is an option for me under certain circumstances.	1	2	3	4	5	6	7	8	9	10
3. My spouse and I agree on major articles of faith.	1	2	3	4	5	6	7	8	9	10
4. We have many friends whose marriages we admire and learn from.	1	2	3	4	5	6	7	8	9	10
5. We are giving our children a religious education.	1	2	3	4	5	6	7	8	9	10
6. I enjoy reading the Bible.	1	2	3	4	5	6	7	8	9	10
7. My spouse and I pray together.	1	2	3	4	5	6	7	8	9	10
8. My spouse and I serve the poor together.	1	2	3	4	5	6	7	8	9	10
9. We enjoy attending church together.	1	2	3	4	5	6	7	8	9	10
10. We pray with our children at home.	1	2	3	4	5	6	7	8	9	10
11. We agree on core values.	1	2	3	4	5	6	7	8	9	10
12. I take time for personal prayer.	1	2	3	4	5	6	7	8	9	10
13. We seek God's will for our lives.	1	2	3	4	5	6	7	8	9	10
14. My spouse sacrifices for our marriage.	1	2	3	4	5	6	7	8	9	10
15. My spouse is a spiritual leader in our home.	1	2	3	4	5	6	7	8	9	10

Name three core values you share with your spouse.
1.
2.
3.

Complete the sentence: When I consider the faith and community that we share in our marriage, I feel _____ because...

Something that I would like to see happen in regards to faith and community is…

Vow Inventory On a scale from 1-10 indicate your level of agreement with the following statements with a 10 = Yes, 5 = Sometimes, and a 1 = No.

	No				Sometimes				Yes	
1. My spouse tells me about what he/she is doing.	1	2	3	4	5	6	7	8	9	10
2. My spouse does not allow any person, place, or thing to be more important than our marriage.	1	2	3	4	5	6	7	8	9	10
3. I do not allow any person, place, or thing to be more important than our relationship.	1	2	3	4	5	6	7	8	9	10
4. My spouse tells me what he/she is thinking.	1	2	3	4	5	6	7	8	9	10
5. My spouse keeps our intimate life private.	1	2	3	4	5	6	7	8	9	10
6. My spouse gives me the space I need to take care of myself.	1	2	3	4	5	6	7	8	9	10
7. My spouse accepts me for who I am and doesn't try to change me.	1	2	3	4	5	6	7	8	9	10
8. I'm a good listener and do not try to always have the last word.	1	2	3	4	5	6	7	8	9	10
9. My spouse shows me great respect and honor.	1	2	3	4	5	6	7	8	9	10
10. My spouse anticipates my needs and helps me.	1	2	3	4	5	6	7	8	9	10
11. My spouse is kind and good to my family.	1	2	3	4	5	6	7	8	9	10
12. My spouse has appropriate boundaries with the opposite sex.	1	2	3	4	5	6	7	8	9	10
13. I struggle with pornography.	1	2	3	4	5	6	7	8	9	10
14. I'm offended when my spouse looks at porn.	1	2	3	4	5	6	7	8	9	10
15. I'm unafraid to raise difficult topics with my spouse.	1	2	3	4	5	6	7	8	9	10
16. My spouse is always ready to resolve differences and apologizes when necessary.	1	2	3	4	5	6	7	8	9	10

When I consider how we try to be faithful to our vows, I feel _____ because…

The Imperfect Couple/Forgiveness Inventory On a scale from 1-10 indicate your level of agreement with the following statements with a 10 = Yes, 5 = Sometimes, and a 1 = No.

	No				Sometimes					Yes
1. My spouse overworks at his/her job.	1	2	3	4	5	6	7	8	9	10
2. I overwork at my job.	1	2	3	4	5	6	7	8	9	10
3. My spouse is happy with his/her work.	1	2	3	4	5	6	7	8	9	10
4. We are both satisfied with the distribution of chores at home.	1	2	3	4	5	6	7	8	9	10
5. We argue over money and how it is spent.	1	2	3	4	5	6	7	8	9	10
6. I am satisfied with the education and training I have received to do my work.	1	2	3	4	5	6	7	8	9	10
7. Clutter at home is a problem for our marriage.	1	2	3	4	5	6	7	8	9	10
8. We make major decisions about our marriage life jointly.	1	2	3	4	5	6	7	8	9	10
9. My spouse is quick to forgive.	1	2	3	4	5	6	7	8	9	10
10. Alcohol abuse is a problem in our marriage.	1	2	3	4	5	6	7	8	9	10
11. Drug abuse is a problem in our marriage.	1	2	3	4	5	6	7	8	9	10
12. Gambling is a problem in our marriage.	1	2	3	4	5	6	7	8	9	10
13. Over-eating is a problem in our marriage.	1	2	3	4	5	6	7	8	9	10
14. My spouse has told me that I am too controlling.	1	2	3	4	5	6	7	8	9	10
15. I trust my spouse to be honest with me.	1	2	3	4	5	6	7	8	9	10
16. My spouse is able to control his/her temper.	1	2	3	4	5	6	7	8	9	10
17. My spouse is critical of me.	1	2	3	4	5	6	7	8	9	10
18. My spouse has been violent with me, either with words or physically attacking me.	1	2	3	4	5	6	7	8	9	10
19. My spouse is able to admit his/her mistakes.	1	2	3	4	5	6	7	8	9	10
20. My spouse is strongly influenced by others.	1	2	3	4	5	6	7	8	9	10

For Reflection:

Identify the ways that you are most likely to hurt your spouse.

_____Negative words   _____Not listening _____Taking her/him for granted

_____Withdrawing _____Avoiding   _____Yelling_____Forgetfulness

_____Undermining agreements _____ Inattentive_____Disregarding feelings

_____Being critical _____Complaining _____Working too much _____Flirting

_____Throwing things or hitting _____Substance abuse _____Withdrawing affection

_____Other _____

Identify the ways that your spouse is most likely to hurt you.

_____Negative words   _____Not listening _____Taking her/him for granted

_____Withdrawing _____Avoiding   _____Yelling_____Forgetfulness

_____Undermining agreements _____ Inattentive_____Disregarding feelings

_____Being critical _____Complaining _____Working too much _____Flirting

_____Throwing things or hitting _____Substance abuse _____Withdrawing affection

_____Other _____

Complete the sentence:

When I think about how we have hurt one another in our marriage and how we work on forgiving one another, I feel_____ because...

A good memory I have of one or both of us asking for forgiveness and being reconciled is...

Something(s) for which I would like to ask for forgiveness is (are)...

Sexual Intimacy Inventory On a scale from 1-10 indicate your level of agreement with the following statements with a 10 = Yes, 5 = Sometimes, and a 1 = No.

	No				Sometimes					Yes
1. I am satisfied with our sex life.	1	2	3	4	5	6	7	8	9	10
2. I was raised with a healthy attitude about sex.	1	2	3	4	5	6	7	8	9	10
3. My spouse is comfortable with his/her sexuality.	1	2	3	4	5	6	7	8	9	10
4. I often prefer intimacy that does not lead to sexual intercourse.	1	2	3	4	5	6	7	8	9	10
5. Romance is alive and well in our marriage.	1	2	3	4	5	6	7	8	9	10
6. I can tell my spouse what I like and dislike in love-making.	1	2	3	4	5	6	7	8	9	10
7. I enjoy sex with my spouse.	1	2	3	4	5	6	7	8	9	10
8. My spouse knows how I like to be touched.	1	2	3	4	5	6	7	8	9	10
9. I am satisfied with how many times we have sex each week.	1	2	3	4	5	6	7	8	9	10
10. We are affectionate with one another outside the bedroom.	1	2	3	4	5	6	7	8	9	10
11. Fear of getting pregnant does not interfere with our sex life.	1	2	3	4	5	6	7	8	9	10
12. We agree on methods of family planning.	1	2	3	4	5	6	7	8	9	10
13. I did not have any bad experiences related to sex as a child or teenager.	1	2	3	4	5	6	7	8	9	10
14. I do not think sexual pleasure is sinful.	1	2	3	4	5	6	7	8	9	10
15. I know what my spouse enjoys during lovemaking.	1	2	3	4	5	6	7	8	9	10
16. Our sexual relationship is mutually pleasurable.	1	2	3	4	5	6	7	8	9	10

Complete the following sentence: When I consider our sexual life I feel _____ because...

Something we could do to strengthen our sexual intimacy is...

Money Inventory On a scale from 1-10 indicate your level of agreement with the following statements with a 10 = Yes, 5 = Sometimes, and a 1 = No.

	No				Sometimes				Yes	
1. We quarrel over money.	1	2	3	4	5	6	7	8	9	10
2. We are able to maintain a budget.	1	2	3	4	5	6	7	8	9	10
3. I am an effective money manager.	1	2	3	4	5	6	7	8	9	10
4. My spouse is an effective money manager.	1	2	3	4	5	6	7	8	9	10
5. We agree on how to balance work with family.	1	2	3	4	5	6	7	8	9	10
6. My spouse earns enough money.	1	2	3	4	5	6	7	8	9	10
7. I have enough money to spend on my personal needs, interests, and hobbies.	1	2	3	4	5	6	7	8	9	10
8. My spouse is a compulsive shopper.	1	2	3	4	5	6	7	8	9	10
9. I am a compulsive shopper.	1	2	3	4	5	6	7	8	9	10
10. The money is "our money," not his or hers.	1	2	3	4	5	6	7	8	9	10
11. Debt is not a problem in our marriage.	1	2	3	4	5	6	7	8	9	10
12. Material possessions are very important to my spouse and me.	1	2	3	4	5	6	7	8	9	10
13. We are able to save for long-term goals.	1	2	3	4	5	6	7	8	9	10
14. I trust my spouse with our money.	1	2	3	4	5	6	7	8	9	10
15. We share our money with people in need.	1	2	3	4	5	6	7	8	9	10
16. I would stay married to my spouse if we were poor.	1	2	3	4	5	6	7	8	9	10

What does money mean to you?

What does money mean to your spouse?

Complete the following sentences:
When I consider our financial situation and the role of money in our marriage I feel _____ because...

Something I think we ought to consider doing to bring greater unity between us in regards to money is...

Protecting Our Holy Communion Worksheet (Copy this page for future use.)

1. Define   the   problem._____

    _____

2. On separate sheets of paper brainstorm solutions.

3. Compare answers; place a <u>checkmark</u> next to those that you like, a <u>question mark</u> next to those that you do not like, but could live with, and an <u>X</u> next to those that you cannot live with.

4. Transfer the answers to the columns below.

5. Discuss the answers in columns A and B; discard column C. Use the X, Y, Z statements and speaker-listener method as needed.

a. We both like it!	b. One of us does not like it, but can live with it!	c. One of us cannot live with it. (These you discard)

6. Your decision is:

7. Your timeframe for re-looking at the issue is:

8. Date, time, and place when you will meet to evaluate how things are going:

The Future Inventory On a scale from 1-10 indicate your level of agreement with the following statements with a 10 = Yes, 5 = Sometimes, and a 1 = No.

	No				Sometimes				Yes	
1. We agree on long-term goals for our future.	1	2	3	4	5	6	7	8	9	10
2. We are satisfied with our preparations for when we retire.	1	2	3	4	5	6	7	8	9	10
3. We are living where we want to live.	1	2	3	4	5	6	7	8	9	10
4. The working spouse(s) is happy with her/his job.	1	2	3	4	5	6	7	8	9	10
5. We have prayed about God's will for our future.	1	2	3	4	5	6	7	8	9	10
6. We have advance directives in the event that illness will leave one of us on life support.	1	2	3	4	5	6	7	8	9	10
7. I am satisfied with where our children are at this stage of their lives.	1	2	3	4	5	6	7	8	9	10
8. I'm not worried about spending more time with my spouse during retirement.	1	2	3	4	5	6	7	8	9	10
9. We have discussed giving more time to serving the poor and elderly.	1	2	3	4	5	6	7	8	9	10
10. We have a list of things we would like to do before we die.	1	2	3	4	5	6	7	8	9	10
11. I am at peace with God and my church.	1	2	3	4	5	6	7	8	9	10
12. My spouse is at peace with God and his/her church.	1	2	3	4	5	6	7	8	9	10
13. There are no family relationships that are strained and need attention.	1	2	3	4	5	6	7	8	9	10
14. We are comfortable with our efforts to care for our aging parents.	1	2	3	4	5	6	7	8	9	10
15. Our burial plans are complete.	1	2	3	4	5	6	7	8	9	10

When I consider our long-term future together, I feel _____ because...

Bibliography

Barry, Dave. *Dave Barry Is from Mars and Venus.* New York, New York: Crown Publishers, 1997.

Chapman, Gary. *The Five Love Languages: How to Express Heartfelt Commitment to Your Mate.* Chicago, Illinois: Northfield Publishing, 1992.

Dobson, James. *Love for a Lifetime: Building a Marriage That Will Go the Distance.* Sisters, Oregon: Multnomah Books, 1987.

Farrel, Bill and Pam. *Red Hot Monogamy: Making Your Marriage Sizzle.* Eugene, Oregon: Harvest House Publishers, 2006.

Feldhahan, Shaunti and Jeff. *For Men Only: A Straightforward Guide to the Inner Lives of Women.* Colorado Springs, Colorado: Multnomah Publishers, 2006.

Feldhahan, Shaunti and Jeff. *For Women Only: A Straightforward Guide to the Inner Lives of Men.* Colorado Springs, Colorado: Multnomah Publishers, 2004.

Gottman, John and Julie. *10 Lessons to Transform Your Marriage.* Atlanta, Georgia: Random House Audio, 2006.

Gray, John. *Why Mars and Venus Collide: Improving Relationships by Understanding How Men and Women Cope Differently with Stress.* New York, New York: Harper Collins Books, 2008.

Haltzman, Scott. *The Secrets of Happily Married Men: Eight Ways to Win Your Wife's Heart Forever.* San Francisco: Jossey-Bass, 2006.

Harley, Willard F. *Love Busters: Protecting Your Marriage from Habits that Destroy Romantic Love.* Grand Rapids, Michigan: Revell, 2008.

Harley, Willard F. *His Needs, Her Needs: Building an Affair-Proof Marriage.* Grand Rapids, Michigan: Revell, 2011.

Harley, Willard F. *Effective Marriage Counseling: The His Needs, Her Needs Guide to Helping Couples.* Grand Rapids, Michigan: Revell, 2010.

Human Sexuality: A Catholic Perspective for Education and Lifelong Learning. Washington D.C. United States Conference of Catholic Bishops, 1990.

Leman, Kevin. *Sex Begins in the Kitchen (Because Love Is an All-Day Affair).* Grand Rapids, Michigan: Fleming H. Revell, 1999.

Markman, Howard J., Stanley, Scott M., Blumberg, Susan L. *Fighting for Your Marriage: The Best-Selling Marriage Enhancement and Divorce Prevention Book.* San Francisco, California: Jossey-Bass, 2001.

Markman, Howard J., Stanley, Scott M., Blumberg, Susan L., Natalie H. Jenkins., Carol Whiteley. *12 Hours to a Great Marriage: A Step-by-Step Guide for Marking Marriage Last.* San Francisco, California: Jossey-Bass, 2004.

Morse, Jennifer Roback. *Love and Economics: Why the Laissesz-Faire Family Doesn't Work.* Dallas, Texas: Spence Publishing Company, 2001.

Morse, Jennifer Roback. *Smart Sex: Finding Lifelong Love in a Hook-up World.* Dallas, Texas: Spence Publishing Company, 2005.

Nelson, Craig. *The First Heroes: The Extraordinary Story of the Doolittle Raid- America's First World War II Victory.* Penguin Books, 2002.

Popcak, Gregory K. *Holy Sex! A Catholic Guide to Toe-Curling, Mind-Blowing, Infallible Loving.* New York, New York: The Crossroad Publishing Company. 2008.

Smith, Robin L. *Lies at the Altar: The Truth about Great Marriages.* New York, New York: Hyperion, 2006.

Szuchman, Paul and Anderson, Jenny. *Spousonomics: Using Economics to Master Love, Marriage, and Dirty Dishes.* New York, New York: Random House, 2011.

Turvey, Matthew D. and Olson, David. *Marriage and Family Wellness: Corporate America's Business?* Minneapolis, Minnesota: The Marriage CoMission, 2006.

Van Epp, John. *How to Avoid Marrying a Jerk: The Foolproof Way to Follow Your Heart without Losing Your Mind.* New York, New York: McGraw Hill, 2006.

Waite, Linda J. and Gallagher, Maggie. *The Case for Marriage: Why Married People Are Happier, Healthier, and Better Off Financially.* New York, New York: Broadway Books, 2000.

Wheat, Ed and Perkins, Gloria Okes. *Love Life for Every Married Couple: How to Fall in Love, Stay in Love, Rekindle Your Love.* Grand Rapids, Michigan: Pyranne Books, 1980.

West, Christopher. *Good News About Sex and Marriage: Answers to Your Honest Questions About Catholic Teaching.* Ann Arbor, Michigan: Servant Publication, 2000.

Yzaguirre, John and Claire-Frazier. *Thriving Marriages: An Inspirational and Practical Guide to Lasting Happiness.* Hyde Park, New York: New City Press, 2005.

Endnotes

[1] *The Case for Marriage,* Linda J. Waite and Maggie Gallagher, Broadway Books, New York, © 2000, pp 13-35.

[2] *Bullseye Marriage: Intentionally Targeting a Great Relationship*, Sara and Francis Fontana, self-published, © 2010, p. 36.

[3] Waite and Gallagher, *The Case for Marriage*, p. 29.

[4] According to the U.S. Census Bureau, 24 million children in America -- one out of three -- live in biological father-absent homes. See http://www.fatherhood.org/media/consequences-of-father-absence-statistics, National Fatherhood Initiative.

[5] Waite and Gallagher, *The Case for Marriage*, p. 31.

[6] Ibid, pp. 82-96.

[7] Ibid, p. 30.

[8] *Marriage and Family Wellness: Corporate America's Business?* Matthew D.Turvey, Psy.D., and David H. Olson, Ph.D., Life Innovations, Minneapolis, Minnesota, © 2006, pp. 6-9.

[9] Waite and Gallagher, *The Case for Marriage*, pp. 124-140.

[10] Ibid. pp. 13-35.

[11] Ibid, p. 29. also see http://www.divorcerate.org/

[12] *12 Hours to a Great Marriage,* Markman, Stanley, Blumberg, Jenkins, and Whiteley, Joseey-Bass publisher, 2004. p. 108.

[13] *Parent Effective Training Workbook,* Kathleen Cornelius and Ralph Jones, Effectiveness Training, Inc, © 1976, p. 14.

[14] Markman, Stanley, Blumberg, Jenkins, and Whiteley, *12 Hours to a Great Marriage*, p. 53.

[15] *Good News About Sex and Marriage*, Christopher West, Servant Publications, Ann Arbor, Michigan, © 2000, p. 22.

[16] *His Needs, Her Needs, Building an Affair-Proof Marriage*, Willard F. Harley, Jr., Revell Books, Grand Rapids, MI © 2011. His list: Sexual fulfillment, recreational companion, attractive spouse, domestic

support, and admiration. Her list: Affection, conversation, honesty, financial stability, involved parent. Harley is talking about patterns for men and women; you may not fit the pattern and arrange the order differently.

[17] *The Five Love Languages: How to Express Heartfelt Commitment to Your Mate*, Gary Chapman, Northfield Publishing, Chicago, © 1995.

[18] Markman, Stanley, Blumberg, Jenkins, and Whiteley, *12 Hours to a Great Marriage,* p. 125.

[19] Age, an inability to conceive a child, and other health-related issues may occasion exceptions to this question. See http://www.marysadvocates.org/syllabus/RiteMarriage.html

[20] see http://www.selfgrowth.com/articles/ *Why Second Marriages Are More Likely to Fail the Challenges of Blending Families*.html, Dr. Richard Nicastro, psychologist and relationship coach.

[21] see http://www.divorce.com/article/divorce-rates-church-attendance

[22] see http://www.edivorcepapers.com/divorce-statistics/christian-divorce-statistics.html

[23] See http://www.nationalcenter.org/MacArthurFarewell.html, General MacArthur's Farewell Speech.

[24] *The First Hero: The Extraordinary Story of Doolittle's Raid*, Craig Nelson, Penguin Books, New York, © 2002, pp. 302-304.

[25] Waite and Gallagher, *The Case for Marriage*, pp. 78-96.

[26] *Sex Begins in the Kitchen: Because Love Is an All-Day Affair*, Dr Kevin Leman, Flemin H. Revell, Grand Rapids, Michigan, © 1999, p. 149.

[27] *Love for a Lifetime: Building a Marriage that Will Go the Distance*, Dr. James Dobson, Multnomah Books, Sisters, Oregon, © 1987, pp. 84-86.

[28] See *"Homosexuality: Nature or Nurture"* Ryan D. Johnson, April 30, 2003, http://allpsych.com/journal/homosexuality.html, "Perhaps there is no one answer, that sexual orientation, whether homosexual or heterosexual; gay, straight, lesbian, or bisexual, all are a cause of a complex interaction between environmental, cognitive, and anatomical factors, shaping the individual at an early age."

[29] See http://gaylife.about.com/od/comingout/a/population.htm. "The Williams Institute at the UCLA School of Law, a sexual orientation law and public policy think tank, estimates that 9 million (about 3.8%) of Americans identify as gay, lesbian, bisexual or transgender (2011). The institute also found that bisexuals make up 1.8% of the population, while 1.7% are gay or lesbian. Transgender adults make up 0.3% of the population."

[30] For information on managing same-sex-attraction issues in marriage go to Homosexual Anonymous (ha-fs.org), Same Sex Attraction (samesexattration.org), and Courage (couragec.net).

[31] *Holy Sex: A Catholic Guide to Toe-Curling, Mind-Blowing, Infallible Loving*, Gregory K. Popcak, Ph.D., Crossroad Publishing, New York, © 2008, p. 23.

[32] *What's in a Number,* Robert Kambic, M.S.H., ttp://www.usccb.org/prolife/issues/nfp/whatsnum.shtml

[33] see http://en.wikipedia.org/wiki/Playgirl, "Mark Graff, President of Trans Digital Media, the brand management firm for Playgirl TV, stated that 50% of *Playgirl's* readership are gay men."

[34] West, *Good News about Sex and Marriage*, p. 19.

[35] Waite and Gallagher, *The Case for Marriage*, pp. 148-149.

Made in the USA
Middletown, DE
07 December 2015